For my parents
Yasmin Khan and Riyaz Talkhani

MY PAST IS A FOREIGN COUNTRY

ZEBA TALKHANI

Kara

SCEPTRE

First published in Great Britain in 2019 by Sceptre
An Imprint of Hodder & Stoughton
An Hachette UK company

2

A CIP catalogue record for this title is available from the British Library

Hardback ISBN 9781473684065
Trade Paperback ISBN 9781473684072
eBook ISBN 9781473684089

Typeset in Sabon by Palimpsest Book Production Limited,
Falkirk, Stirlingshire

Printed and bound in Great Britain by Clays Ltd, Elcograf S.p.A.

Hodder & Stoughton policy is to use papers that are natural, renewable and
recyclable products and made from wood grown in sustainable forests. The logging
and manufacturing processes are expected to conform to the environmental
regulations of the country of origin.

Hodder & Stoughton Ltd
Carmelite House
50 Victoria Embankment
London EC4Y 0DZ

www.sceptrebooks.co.uk

Prologue

I was four when I ran away from home for the second time. The first time, a police officer found me and brought me home, along with a big packet of crisps and a softie ice cream. I do not know how he figured out where I lived or whom I belonged to. I did not speak a word of Arabic and had no sense of direction. I think he must have had some help from the building caretakers in the area. The second time, the ordeal lasted much longer.

We lived in an apartment building in Jeddah at the time and Mama opened the door to drop something off at our neighbours', the ones who lived in a flat opposite ours. I saw my chance and slipped out from behind her. There were four flats on each floor and the building had a caretaker. In Saudi Arabia, a caretaker is called a *haris*, which roughly translates from Arabic to 'lion' or 'guardian'. Every apartment building in Jeddah that we lived in had a *haris*. A wall and a main gate surrounded our building and the front porch was a safe place to play in.

It was a hot afternoon and when I reached the main entrance of the building, my feet faltered. On the chair by the door, the *haris* was sitting with a cap over his face. Maybe he was sleeping. I decided to risk it and took a few steps towards the gate. Just when I thought I had managed my escape, an arm caught me by the wrist and pulled me back. I screamed. The *haris* laughed. He asked me something in Arabic. I replied in Urdu. I felt understood when I explained how I was leaving home because my parents did not love me any more, that they loved my younger brother Raiyan a lot more. He nodded sympathetically and patted the granite step beside his chair. I sat down.

Mama and Raiyan were a couple of floors above and Papa was at work. I missed the people who surrounded me in India. Jeddah felt lonely. Time passed in silence and I got bored. The *azaan* (usually heard from the minaret of a mosque) filled the silence with its call for the afternoon prayer. The *haris* stood up and asked me to follow him. He knocked on the door of a flat on the ground floor of the building. A man opened the door and they exchanged greetings. The flight of stairs leading up to Mama and Raiyan was beside this man's door.

I decided it was time to go back home. But the *haris* had different plans. When I tried to pull away, his grip tightened around my wrist and he pulled me inside the flat with him. Once inside, I noticed the flat was nothing like ours. There was a smell to this space I will never forget. A mix of burned meat, body odour and *qahwa*, an Arabic coffee infused with cardamom. The sofa faced away from the main door and the windows were plastered with black sheets, making it impossible to tell whether it was night or day. The men served themselves *qahwa* and the *haris* offered me something to eat; I cannot remember if it was a biscuit or a packet of crisps. I refused the offer.

I wanted to be let out but was not sure how to ask the men to unlock the door for me. When the *haris* patted the sofa beside him, I did not move. I hoped that by staying close to the door, I could communicate my need to pass through it. While the men continued speaking, I considered throwing a tantrum, but something warned me to not make these men angry.

I do not remember much from those years in that apartment building, but the floor plan of this stranger's house is imprinted in my memory. Whenever I come across that stale smell I remember the fear I felt that day and how the minutes stretched ahead of me. I remained silent and did not voice my desire to escape.

After what felt like hours, there was a knock on the door. It was loud and incessant. The men were not expecting anyone. They stood up and the *haris* came to the door while I stayed close, waiting for the right moment to escape from behind him. It was our neighbour, the one who lived opposite us. I need not have worried about making my escape because she was there for me. She shouted at the *haris* for his irresponsible behaviour. The *haris* shrugged his shoulders and let me pass. I ran into our neighbour's arms. She took me upstairs to where Mama was standing by our open front door, crying. I could not wait to be in her arms, to feel safe again. When I saw her, I slid out of my neighbour's arms and ran towards Mama. But before I could get too far, the neighbour grabbed me and slapped me across the face. 'Never run away from home,' she scolded. 'Do you know how worried your mother was?' she asked. Mama watched in silence.

Mama's silence was a big part of my early years and this silence cost us both. This book, too, is as much about Mama's silences as it is about my words, and the lingering discordance this caused.

It is this discordance that I write about here and it is this discordance that has driven me and shaped me, the inability to look away, to ignore, to forget, to be mollified, and to believe that nothing out of the ordinary has happened, is happening.

Part One
Sirsi, Honnavar and Jeddah

One of my earliest childhood memories is of Mama shielding her thoughts and memories from me. Despite her best efforts, I managed to steal from Mama three stories about my birth that are dear to me. The first story is about my uncle, Mama's eldest brother. She once told me about how he woke up before dawn every morning, filled a thermos with a hot drink and took a short cut through the fields to get to the hospital where Mama was recovering from my birth. He stayed with her for a while each morning, making sure she had everything she needed before heading to the bank where he worked as a clerk.

Though she mentioned it in her retelling, I have forgotten what it was that he brought her in that thermos and I am too afraid to ask. Memories are precarious by nature and I am scared that Mama might take this story back from me, deny it ever happened, tell me I am misremembering.

The second story is a fact. My name was Aisha before it was Zeba. It was Mama's wish to have a daughter named Aisha. After my birth, when Mama revealed my name to the rest of the family, her mother-in-law, my dadi, told Mama that I would grow up to be mentally unstable like another Aisha known to the family. Mama decided not to risk it and changed my name to Zeba. Growing up, I thought of Aisha as an invisible twin. She was the prettier one, she had great hair, she wore beautiful dresses, and she was Mama's favourite. Often I would wonder what life would be like if I was her.

A year ago, when I brought up this story and asked Mama

the identity of the original Aisha, she was aghast. 'Do not write about that,' she exclaimed. When I pushed for details, she minimised the story and said that her elder sister was keen to name me Zeba. Mama said that the moment it became clear that I could not be Aisha, her sister came forward with the suggestion and I was renamed immediately. Her retelling didn't explain why I couldn't be named Aisha.

'You were Aisha only for a few moments, and for the *azaan*,' Mama assured me. It is an Islamic practice to whisper the *azaan*, the call to prayer, into the newborn's ears soon after birth. During the first *azaan* that a Muslim baby hears, they are addressed by their name. While Mama was keen for me to forget my alter ego, all I could think was that my first *azaan* was not mine.

The third story involves my mother's mother, my nani. Apparently as a newborn, I could not stop looking around me. Nani watched me follow the voices in the hospital room when I was just a couple of days old. When Nani noticed the way I was following the damp patterns on the ceiling, she told Mama that one day I would travel the world, that I had a curiosity about me that was unusual. Mama told me this story when I was a child and Nani repeated it when I told her I was going to the UK for my master's. 'I always knew you were meant for great things,' she said in Urdu, when I told her about my scholarship. I remember feeling relieved when Nani narrated the story exactly as Mama had. I was not ready to lose another memory to my family's inability to recollect.

These stories were rare and trickled down to me over the years, with much effort from my end. Growing up, when I asked Mama about her life before marriage, I got nothing from her. When I asked her how her newly married life was, I got a blank stare. When I asked her how she knew that Papa was the one for her, she scolded me for asking offensive questions. Once I asked her how long she was in labour for with me. She said 'too long' and left the room in a huff.

She had similar reactions when I asked about her own childhood; she never gave anything away and was quick to cut Papa short when he tried to fill in the blanks for me. My parents' families are related. This meant that they had a few shared memories from their childhood. Over the years, and despite Mama's best efforts, Papa let slip stories about Mama's epic tantrums, her special way of terrorising her elder brothers (Papa once walked in on a seven-year-old Mama pinning one brother to the wall) and her reputation for being the most beautiful girl in her college. This last story involved a blue dress, but it is only recently that Mama indulged the retelling. The last time I was home, I asked to hear the story again. Papa obliged. The most beautiful blue dress that made her stand out from all the other girls in Sirsi. Instead of asking him to stop, she wistfully recollected the shade of blue. Aquamarine. It caught the sun and shimmered lightly when she moved. Papa concurred. The style was unique too, an *anarkali* cut which was new to Sirsi. There was no dress like it. Soon after she bought the dress, other girls in her college had similar dresses made for themselves. A trendsetter, my Mama.

Mama comes from a small town in the South Indian state of Karnataka called Sirsi. It is a beautiful town, surrounded by forest. During my early years, we visited India every summer and spent most of our two-month break in Honnavar, my father's hometown.

Every year, Mama spent a week or two with her parents in Sirsi. I enjoyed watching Mama turn into the youngest child of the family. Watching her brothers get her favourite sweets for her and her mother, my nani, cooking her childhood meals. Mama loves peanuts and her brothers always remembered to pick up a packet of freshly roasted ones on his way from the bank. After dinner, we all sat on the living-room floor and spread newspapers around us. This was to catch the shells. The elders poured little hills of peanuts in front of each child. We then spent the evening chatting in front of the TV and conquering our individual hills. Fights would break out when I tried to steal from my brother or my younger cousins.

Sirsi and Honnavar are around three hours away from each other by road. The road trip meant driving through the Western Ghats, the lush mountains that spread across the southwestern coast of India. The Western Ghats are a UNESCO World Heritage Site and the views are breathtaking, with misty skies and endless green expanses. Streams and waterfalls add beauty to the landscape. Driving through the Ghats means winding roads with sharp turns through hills and valleys.

As a child, I looked forward to these car journeys between Honnavar and Sirsi. The Ghats are home to a thriving wild-life, including snakes and predatory cats. I remember seeing snakes slither across the road, but others in the family have seen tigers, leopards and Indian bison. The winding roads are lined by forests on either side and as we visited India in the monsoon season, it usually rained on these road trips.

The Sirsi home was a real 'joint' family, with three gen-erations living under one roof. The house belonged to Mama's grandfather and eventually her father, my nana. It is the same house my nani moved to as a young bride. It is the house in which she gave birth to four children and where she cared for her ailing in-laws. Nana, my maternal grandfather, is one of six siblings, but only three of them remained in Sirsi. At some point during my early years, there was a dispute between Nana and his brother which led to them building a wall to separate the family. I remember spending time with Mama's cousins every year and suddenly we stopped seeing them. This lasted for a few years. On our side of the wall lived Nana and Nani, their two sons, their two daughters-in-law, their six grandchildren and Nana's spinster sister. We call her Phappu.

Phappu had a room of her own near the kitchen, a big space with no windows. I wonder if this was her childhood room. Every inch of the room was hidden under the weight of her possessions. The door to this room remained shut to the children of the house and sometimes Phappu would even lock the door to keep us out. The space was sacred. Even as a child I knew not to cross the threshold without her permission, not out of fear but out of love.

Anytime anyone in the house needed something, we would go to Phappu. If she could not find what we needed in her room (a rare occurrence), she would put on her burka and rush out to get it for us. As a child, I never registered that she was my nana's sister. When the children spoke to her, we did not use the respectful pronouns reserved for the other elders in the house. Neither did Mama or her siblings.

I never questioned Phappu's place there. She was always an integral part of the Sirsi home and our family. It was not until many years later, just before my twenty-first birthday, that I thought to ask the question. It was my first night in Cambridge, where I was about to start my master's. Papa, as was customary for him, accompanied me on my first trip to this new place. We were in a hotel lobby, unwilling to go out and face the cold January rain. While we waited for the clouds to clear, I broached the subject of our family. I suppose being so many miles away from all the people we loved made it easier to talk about them.

'Why did Phappu never marry?' I asked.

'She did marry,' Papa responded.

This was news to me. I sat up straighter, forgetting to lean towards the fireplace.

'What happened?'

Her husband died after a year of their marriage. His family failed to mention that he had cancer. Phappu and her family did not find out until after the wedding. Her husband was not involved in this betrayal, apparently. It was the era of arranged marriages and they did not get to speak before their wedding day.

'He was good to her,' Papa said. 'She loved him and they were happy together. It was her mother-in-law who was the problem.'

'What happened then?'

'Nothing really, he passed away a year after they married and she came back home and never left. She didn't want to remarry.'

I left Papa in the hotel lobby and walked to my dorm. On my first night in my new room, I cried for my Phappu. I cried for her loss and I cried for the silence surrounding it. I wondered if she still thought about her husband and if she thought about how different her life would be were he alive. I wondered if she imagined having her own grandchildren instead of running errands for her brother's family.

Nana, my maternal grandfather, is a shopkeeper and there was a lot of joy in that little corner shop. The shop had its own rituals and was set a few feet above street level. Because of this height difference, we sat cross-legged on cushions to remain at eye-level with the customers who stopped by. I waited eagerly for them to order candies, chocolate, fudge, toffees or home-made biscuits by weight so I could use the magnificent scales that sat in the middle of the shop. I enjoyed lifting the weights, how they felt on my palm, and the creaking of the scales. I was quick with my calculations and awaited the pat on the back when I got it right. I loved handing little paper packets of sweets to schoolchildren on their way home.

The shop was run by Nana and his youngest son. They took turns to sit behind the till. After lunch Nana went home for a nap and my uncle allowed me to sit behind the till and play at being a shopkeeper. The till was an antique wooden box with a small slit on the top left corner to drop coins in. If the customer required change, the box was unlocked. The little square under the slit was where all kinds of coins were dropped and when the shop was quiet, the person behind the till got to arrange the coins in the right squares. This was the job I most cherished and I would find excuses to keep opening the box and making sure all the money was still there.

Papa did not usually stay in Sirsi the whole time we were there. He either dropped us off or joined us for a couple of nights at the end of our trip. One morning, when I was around six years old, I had my breakfast at home and got ready to go to the shop. This was the only walk I was allowed to take on my own, as the route was in full view of all the neighbours who knew who I was and where I was meant to go.

On this particular day, I was talking to myself and taking huge bites from a jam and ghee sandwich my Nani had made especially for this seven-minute walk when I spotted my father at the entrance. This was unexpected. I broke into a run and scrambled over the threshold of the shop, breathless. I was feeling an intense need to introduce him to what I considered my turf. I was so happy to see him. When I ended my monologue and fell to the cushioned floor with a sigh, I thought of all the chocolates I could eat and how happy I was to see Papa. I distinctly remember the joy I felt. When I try to remember a happy memory, this is the first one that comes to mind. Sirsi is full of such beautiful memories.

Mama too was a happy person in Sirsi. She was carefree, and motherhood did not turn into its usual performance. She teased me and played with me. She indulged my endless questions and did not worry about mealtimes because she knew that I looked forward to eating with my cousins. At her parents' house, no one was judging her or waiting for her to fail. There was no anxiety or unrest surrounding Mama in Sirsi. She stayed in her childhood room for that week and sometimes caught up with old friends. The children all slept in the living room, our mattresses rolled out next to each other, making bedtime a lively affair with stories from our grandmother.

Sirsi was just one small part of our yearly trip to India. Most of the holiday we stayed in Honnavar, and in the early 2000s, when Dada, my paternal grandfather, was appointed Chairman of the Karnataka Minorities Development Corporation (KMDC), we spent more time in their government flat in Bangalore. The KMDC's aim was to serve the disadvantaged minorities in the state of Karnataka, and this was Dada's second career, after years of being a successful lawyer in Honnavar.

Our summer breaks usually lasted a little over two months, from June to August each year. I do not remember a single school holiday when we were not in India. Even when we went on family vacations to other countries, Papa always made sure that we ended these trips in India. The rest of the year, we stayed in Jeddah.

As a child, my curiosity knew no bounds. I did not care for the age-appropriate animated movies my parents bought on VHS for me and my brother. I was more interested in the Indian TV shows that my parents watched in the evenings. I focused on the adults around me and I was always listening in, trying to put things together, trying to figure out their intentions. The Indian soap operas of that time focused heavily on the conflict between mothers-in-law and daughters-in-law. I watched avidly as the women battled it out at home and manipulated the men of the family to take sides. It was the woman's job to make a place for herself in her angry husband's heart, to win the trust of her indifferent father-in-law and become friends with her sister-in-law. All this while not letting her spirit be crushed repeatedly by her mother-in-law. Some shows even had a 'vamp'.

The vamp was particularly interesting to me. She was the woman in love with the protagonist's husband. This character was usually introduced as a plot device to unite the daughter-in-law and mother-in-law. Sometimes she was brought in by the mother-in-law herself, as revenge against the woman who 'stole' her son from her. You could tell a vamp by her makeup and the special soundtrack that played every time she was on-screen. She was the homewrecker, unmarried herself but inter-ested in other women's husbands. She looked like the only one having any fun in life. I figured early on that the best way to avoid the hassles of adulthood was to remain unmarried. Safe in this knowledge, I continued watching women suffer on-screen and off-screen.

These shows also set fashion trends in India and people watched them as much for the latest styles in clothes, jewel-lery and makeup as for the story. A recurring plot device was killing the main character and then bringing them back post-plastic surgery but not revealing their identity for months. My favourite game was to try to guess which dead person the new character was. These soap operas were a crash course in storytelling and I loved the dramatic turns they took almost every week.

Off-screen, I noticed similar trends but on a less dramatic (and glamorous) scale. I was obsessed with Mama's every move and watched her like a hawk, almost as though someone set me up to do just this. From a young age, even before my conscious memories emerged, I apparently wanted to know everything about Mama. My curiosity scared her and it's probably what caused her to remain guarded around me throughout my childhood.

While Papa encouraged and indulged my curiosity, Mama tried her best to protect herself from my prying nature. She censored herself around me and warned others to do the same. She would point discreetly in my direction and whisper 'antenna' so they would know not to blurt out anything sensitive in my presence. Even when I did a great job of pretending to mind my own business, my face buried in a book, she knew.

My eavesdropping was so legendary that Mama and Papa had to speak in Kannada with each other to keep things from me. Kannada is one of the languages of Karnataka. The language does not share similarities with either Urdu or English (the two languages I speak). However, my observations were so keen that I could often figure out exactly what they were discussing.

My brother exploited my talent often. When our parents spoke to each other in Kannada, he would turn to me and ask, '*Kya baat kar rahen, didi?*' What are they saying? I would then loudly 'translate' and watch Mama's expressions. From her silent reactions, I could tell if I was right or wrong. If I was right, I turned to Raiyan and smiled. If I was wrong, I shook my head at my brother, gestured at him to wait, and continued listening.

The more Mama protected her thoughts and words, the more I wanted them to be revealed. Papa remembers my obsession with Mama. I knew I was an attention-seeking child and assumed that I troubled both my parents equally. But in a recent conversation Papa clarified that my strong, almost possessive streak was only reserved for Mama. That it was only her attention I craved, even before I could speak. Apparently, I needed to know at all times her location in relation to mine. I made it difficult for her to socialise at gatherings by climbing over her intricate Indian dresses, perhaps damaging them in the process, and placing my face inches away from hers, making it impossible for her to see anyone but me.

When I was a bit older, I remember Mama telling me that I could never see her happy when I was a child. I think she was referring to how I reacted to her socialising with family and friends. This hurt, especially because I had no memories of what she was accusing me of. I nurtured this hurt tenderly and carefully throughout my years at home. I felt misunderstood by Mama and unable to defend my intentions, especially because I had no memory of these incidents. I felt as though Mama was being unreasonable and I expected her to forgive me because she was the adult. Many years later, after I had left home, Mama told me that she was too self-conscious as a new mother and that every innocent action of mine embarrassed her when around other people. She apologised without apologising, by retelling the stories in a way that was more kind to me than the previous versions. She admitted that it was heartening to be loved so deeply by her firstborn.

It was easier to follow Mama around as a child because we had a traditional home set-up: Mama stayed home to take care of us, while Papa went out to work. He worked in the power division of a large company and it fascinated me that this company was older than Saudi Arabia. I later learned that the company was not founded by one of the desert tribes that became part of Saudi Arabia but by a family in the neighbouring country of Bahrain. Papa has been with the same company since 1996.

Mama managed the household, starting her day an hour before everyone else. She cooked for us, did our laundry, kept a clean house and made sure we completed our homework.

During my early years, the more Mama cooked, the less I ate. Mama still shudders at the memories of my eating habits. When I was a baby, Mama fed me double the specified amount of food and these mealtimes often ended with me throwing up in my highchair. I have no memory of this, but Papa once nonchalantly mentioned two details from this time that struck me as odd. One, the fact that Mama overfed me. The second that she took it personally when I did not eat my food.

As if to add insult to injury, I would eat when others fed me. I wonder if it was body memory that made me wary of Mama's attempts to feed me as I grew into a toddler. I cannot imagine how it must feel to be obsessively fed long after you are full. Mothers in my community face unique pressures to conform to the 'correct' way of raising a child. There are too many people waiting in the wings to point out their mistakes. Mama was all of twenty-three when I was born and of a susceptible nature.

When I was around four years old, one of Papa's colleagues' wife told Mama that I should be scared into eating. Apparently, her own daughter used to be a fussy eater, but not any more. At this point, Mama was desperate for any help she could get. The woman told Mama to switch on the gas stove and heat a stainless steel spoon on the fire. The key was to make sure that I was watching. Mama followed the instructions.

She sat me down on a chair by the kitchen door. She switched on the stove. She picked up a spoon and held it to the flames. 'Look, Zeba,' she said. 'This is a hot spoon and if you do not eat everything on your plate, I will burn your skin and it will hurt.' I am not sure if she actually said any of this but the threat was effectively communicated to me.

There are two sides to this story and I cannot always tell which fragments are mine and which belong to Mama's memory. I do not remember the flames or the spoon. I do not remember her walking towards me with this heated spoon. However, I do remember a layer of black soot on the spoon. I remember both my wrists locked in Mama's hand and I remember my need to get away from her. Then I remember a layer of spoon-shaped skin blackening and tearing away from my thigh. I do not remember if I finished everything on my plate that day.

Whenever we revisit the story, Mama is always sorry that it happened. She insists that she never intended to hurt me. That the trick was meant to scare me. That fear was all she was trying to elicit. I remember wiggling; I remember causing Mama to lose her balance. I remember us both crying.

What I had forgotten, though, was how I waited all day for Papa to return from work and followed him to his bedroom where he was changing out of his office clothes. While he rummaged in the cupboard, I perched up on the edge of the bed, lifted my oversized t-shirt and said, 'Look what Mama did to me today.' Mama was not around, so I know this is not her memory that I have made mine. I know I was tattling because when Papa asked me if I was in pain, I distinctly remember not feeling any pain in the moment but deciding to lie about it anyway. I remember making this choice. I told him I was in a lot of pain and pulled at the dead skin to show him the full damage.

Though I have discussed the events of that day with Mama, we have never discussed the consequences of my tattling on her. In fact, I was reminded of my act only recently when Mama shared an anecdote about her friend who lived in fear of her mother-in-law, who treated her like a servant. One day, after hours of cooking and cleaning and with her mother-in-law away on a family engagement, Mama's friend decided to watch TV. This was not something she would dare to do in the presence of her in-laws.

Just as she settled on the couch, her four-year-old son walked in. He saw what his mother was doing and he recognised immediately that she was doing something she shouldn't be. 'Wait till I tell Dadi, you will be in so much trouble,' he said, while his mother scrambled to switch off the TV.

Immediately the memory of my tattling on Mama came back to me. I was struck by how children discern power dynamics. Up until then, I believed that my fraught relationship with Mama was because of how she policed me. But I think it had something to do with both of us policing each other. That is the beauty of the patriarchy, I suppose; the ones being policed are the ones policing.

There were a considerable number of Indian men working at Papa's office and our families met socially at weekends. During my childhood, many of these gatherings took place at our homes – the culture of meeting at restaurants did not start until I was a teenager. The brunt of cooking for these endless parties fell on Mama and there was a time when we hosted over twenty families, sometimes more. Looking back, it feels as though Mama spent her twenties and thirties cooking for people she did not know.

The parties were not simple affairs. Mama made at least ten dishes and in large quantities. A detail that differed from parties hosted by other families was the fact that Mama never ate with the guests. She always had dinner after everyone had left and most of the dishes were washed and dried. She would then pile her plate with some leftovers and sit alone in the living room with the TV on. We were not allowed to watch TV at mealtimes, but this was the only exception.

At these parties, the food was served buffet style on the dining table. The men helped themselves first and moved to the main living room. The women helped themselves after the men and children and they usually stayed confined to the second, smaller living room. When we had too many people, the women spilled out into our bedrooms too. I enjoyed these parties as it gave me a chance to play with other children. I loved the food and I loved it when the guests praised Mama's cooking and she accepted the compliments with shy nods. She seemed truly happy in those moments, but I could never forget the anxiety and stress she exuded in the hours leading up to these parties.

On the morning of one of these gatherings, Mama caught her finger in a hand mixer and there was blood everywhere. Raiyan and I ran out of our rooms when we heard her cry out. We found her in the kitchen, amidst an array of pots. I panicked but Raiyan took over. He was barely eight years old. He told me to call Papa while he held Mama's hand and walked her out of the kitchen. I had never seen Mama in pain before. I dialled Papa's number and asked him to come home. When I found Raiyan and Mama again, they were in her bedroom; Mama was sitting on the bed, Raiyan standing beside her. He had found some cotton and bandages and was trying to blot the heavy blood flow. I stood by the door, feeling helpless.

Mama pulled her hand away from Raiyan's grip and fell back on the bed, her body convulsing. I do not remember anything else from that day except that the party went on as planned, sans one dish. That evening I watched Mama even more closely than usual. I could not believe that just a few hours ago this elegant, beautifully made up woman was wailing and withering. It was the first of many times that I was in absolute awe of her ability to perform the role that society had forced upon her. I still feel a sharp sting when I ask myself why the party was not cancelled that day.

* * *

Raiyan and I went to the same school in Jeddah, but never met on campus because our school was segregated based on the gender binary. Mama woke me up at 6 a.m. and got me ready for school. At 7 a.m. Papa woke up. At 8 a.m. it was Raiyan's turn to wake up. The boys and girls sections of our school had their own separate buildings and resources, but they shared the fleet of school buses, almost 100 of them. I think this was the main reason for the different start times. The bus that collected me every morning was the same bus that came to pick up Raiyan a couple of hours later.

During the day, Mama stayed home to cook lunch and dinner, tidy the house, tackle laundry and catch up on sleep when needed. This was brought up often in conversations within the community: how lucky women are to be home all day and sleep as much as they want to. The efforts that went into single-handedly raising children and keeping a good home without the privilege of free mobility was never acknowledged during my childhood. There were many instances of husbands not wanting their wives to work while remarking on how lucky their wives were to not have to work. One of my favourite teachers resigned midway through the academic year because her husband demanded that she do so. We knew each other socially and I once overheard him complaining that all his wife did was talk on the phone, watch TV or sleep when he was hard at work in the office. It made me so angry to see that in private he was controlling his wife's actions and in public he was deriding her for her inaction.

I came home from school at 2 p.m. every day. When Raiyan was in nursery, he was home by noon and waited for me to get back from school before eating his lunch. Once he graduated to primary school, I did not see him until 4 p.m.

Papa came home around 6 p.m. or later, almost always tired from the day's slog. He then took us out to our appointments or errands.

*   *   *

When I was five, Mama, Raiyan and I spent the better part of the year in Honnavar while Papa remained in Jeddah. I think this was for financial reasons. When I asked Papa about this recently, he said he wanted to do something nice for his parents by giving them time with their grandchildren.

The year I spent in Honnavar as a child was a beautiful one. The house itself was a thing of dreams, with many rooms, dark hallways, dusty attics and fully stuffed pantries. My father and his four brothers were born in this house. My paternal grandmother, Dadi, ran the household with the help of Saju Khala (a woman who had worked with the family since my father was a young boy), Shakila (a young girl whose parents sent her to work for my family with the understanding that my grandparents would take responsibility for her marriage when she came of age) and Francis, our driver. There were others who came and went; memorable among them were Tasneem, Samiyya, Salma and Bibi.

The house was in a walled compound, roughly 17,000 square feet in size, with the house taking up one-fifth of the land. The rest of the land was taken up by an abandoned wooden shed and a guesthouse which was sometimes rented out. During my father's childhood, the shed housed a buffalo. There was also a chicken pen and every morning someone would retrieve warm eggs for breakfast. We shared this outdoor space with a Dalmatian dog named Tiger. There were many coconut trees surrounding the house and flowers in the front garden and fruit trees in the backyard. My favourite tree to climb was the water apple tree by the back door. Regardless of where I am in the world, every time I smell jasmine I am taken back to Honnavar and helping Dadi water the garden. I was the only one allowed to pluck the flowers, which I either presented to Dadi or asked to have pinned to my hair.

Raiyan started speaking when he was three, but his words

were incomprehensible for a while longer. During this time, I became Raiyan's official translator. Every time he spoke, I would repeat what he meant. He was happy with my interpretations and never refuted them, even if I was not entirely correct. In fact, he got into the habit, even as a young adult, of turning to me and saying, '*Haina, didi*?' (Am I right, sister?) whenever he spoke at length.

Like me, Raiyan also ran away from home when he was little. While this habit was slapped out of me, nothing seemed to work on him. In Honnavar, there were too many open doors and not enough ways to confine him. Sometimes neighbours found him in the fish market by the Sharavathi River and brought him home. Another time a lorry driver found him in the middle of the road. Once Saju Khala's daughter-in-law found him in her backyard and waited for my family to come and fetch him. That day Raiyan came back home with kohl around his eyes, a ritual that was meant to ward off evil eye.

Raiyan's habit of running away caused a lot of worry. Dada bought metres of thick rubber strips to tie around the back and front gates of the house to stop Raiyan from escaping. The adults struggled with this contraption and most visitors took to shouting out to us for help with getting in and out. Ironically, it stopped everyone except Raiyan, who climbed the gates and jumped to the other side instead. Everyone in the house was alert and kept an eye on Raiyan. Even Tiger joined in and took to barking loudly every time Raiyan got close to either of the gates. The panic surrounding his escapes seeped into my consciousness too and often I would dream about losing my brother and him growing up with the fisherwomen and forgetting all about me. To do my bit to stop him from running away, I took to spending more time playing with him and keeping him entertained with stories.

I was an avid storyteller from a young age and though I

had many listeners in Honnavar, Raiyan was the most enthusiastic of them all. He just could not get enough of my stories
and would always ask, '*Phir kya hua, Didi?*' What happened
next? He asked this with such earnestness and missed the
jokes so often that I did not have the heart to tell him that
the story was long over and now I was simply making
up things so as not to disappoint him.

This storytelling was also encouraged by Dadi, my paternal
grandmother. In Honnavar we had a large swing in the
main entrance of the house. I liked to sit on it with her and
Raiyan and tell them stories about flying fishes and warrior
princesses. When I got stuck, Dadi would ask questions that
would help me develop my story and take it to different
realms. I would hold tight to the chains locking the swing
to the ceiling and sit beside Dadi while Raiyan hung
from the other corner and listened with his mouth open. I
enjoyed this attention and sought it often.

I also remember owning a fancy umbrella hat that I liked
to wear to school when it rained. It was exactly like an
umbrella (mine was rainbow-coloured) but instead of a stick
to hold it, there was a tight headband which meant I was
protected from the rain while remaining hands-free. I showed
off my hands-free-ness as much as I could when I had the
umbrella hat on, gesturing wildly and talking loudly all
the way to school and back.

Saju Khala and Raiyan came to drop me off, with Tiger
following a few steps behind us. I was embarrassed by this
entourage and every few minutes I turned back and tried to
shoo Tiger away. He waited for a little while and then
continued following us. I also tried to leave Raiyan at home
but he was always ready before me and waited by the gate to
drop me off. It was impossible to get out of the house without
him noticing. He came again at lunchtime with the driver or
Shakila.

My uncle's wedding is my last memory of that time in Honnavar. The entire family descended on us and the house was no longer just my playground. I don't remember much from the wedding celebrations themselves, but I do remember accompanying the women in my family to 'see girls' for my uncle in the months leading up to this wedding. As arranged marriages are prevalent in my community, the culture of visiting a potential bride's home to 'see' her is common practice. My family would have seen several girls, but this is the only one I remember. On the day of the visit, someone told me that we were going to my future auntie's house. I was excited. When we arrived, she was nowhere in sight. I remember my family getting impatient. I willed her to come down the stairs; I worried her tardiness would be held against her.

When she finally made her way to the living room, she was dressed in a bright yellow *salwar kurta* with a matching scarf draped over her head. She walked with her face down and sat primly across from us. I saw the women in my family look at each other and crinkle their noses. I don't know how long this lasted, but soon the girl was excused and she went to the kitchen. '*Bohut kali hai*,' they said. She is too dark. Dadi handed me some money and asked me to give it to the bride who wouldn't be my auntie. When I found her in the kitchen, she was laughing with her head back. I remember this because I think it was the first time I saw a woman laugh so openly. When I handed her the money, she patted my head and went back to talking to her sisters. I noticed that her colour was the same as mine. Did this mean I was *kali* too? This is the earliest memory I have of not being beautiful enough. I was five years old.

I have no memories of Mama from these months in Honnavar.

* * *

After coming back to Jeddah, I was enrolled in the Indian school where I studied for the next ten years, from 1996 to 2006. I was expecting to return to the old flat but during our absence, Papa had moved us to a two-bed flat in a compound of sorts, six buildings surrounded by a common wall. It was not a conventional compound as the gates were never shut and there was no security. There were two caretakers in charge of the six buildings. Most of the tenants in these buildings were Indian families with children my age. Though the flat was bigger than the previous one and there were opportunities to go out and play in the afternoon, it was still a change from the big house and garden in Honnavar.

I imagine Mama's life changed drastically too. She was in charge of her family again. The household chores kept Mama busy, but they also limited her interaction with the outside world. When I returned from school, Mama asked me to tell her about my day. She didn't accept grunts and shrugs as appropriate responses and often I ended up relaying my entire day to her in detail. Through my stories, Mama became invested in the lives of the people I met at school and this daily exercise made me observe the people around me more keenly.

In Jeddah, Raiyan continued to find ways to escape, though he never went too far. On his first day of school, while Papa was unlocking the car, Raiyan hopped on the bus that had stopped to pick up the other students from the neighbourhood. By the time Papa realised where he was, the bus was already on its way. Papa had to drive behind the bus, following its meandering route all the way to school so he could get Raiyan registered and take him to his new class.

Papa had vertical metal grills drilled into the window frames to discourage Raiyan from jumping out. One afternoon Mama entered her bedroom to find Raiyan hanging outside the window, using the grills as monkey bars, his trademark grin plastered on his face. 'Enjoying the wind,' he later explained to me. The same day a blacksmith came and welded lopsided horizontal grills across the original grills.

Our living area was the bedroom I shared with Raiyan. It was a large space with a double bed, two sofas, a big black desk that Papa built for us, a wardrobe that I shared with Raiyan and a TV in the corner. We ate our dinners on the floor in this room and then spent time there as a family until bedtime. The formal living room was reserved for hosting guests.

Sometimes Raiyan and I dared to switch on the TV at night but most channels were unavailable that late. In the day, my parents made us watch BBC World News to help us improve our English. We were encouraged to look up unfamiliar words in a tattered copy of *The Chambers Dictionary*. When we were bored of the BBC, we pretended to be news reporters ourselves, and in tight-lipped accents repeated the gossip from the compound to each other and sometimes to Mama as she laughed helplessly. The only time we watched in silence was when Princess Diana died. I cried, Raiyan kept going close to the TV and Papa had to keep pulling him back.

The news channels kept showing the car crash scene on a loop and we could not look away. For a long while after her death, every time we drove through an underpass near the centre of Jeddah, Raiyan would sit up straight and declare that this was where Princess Diana died. In our family, we still refer to it as the Princess Diana underpass.

At some weekends we went to Azziziyah, a South Asian area. My school was located in this area and most of my classmates lived nearby too. Though we moved homes every few years and we visited this area often, my parents never chose to live there. When I was younger, I was fascinated by this place and wanted to be closer to my friends. To feel like I was in India when I was not, was a good feeling. The women there seemed to share a little more freedom than other expat women because of the community they had built together and the familiarity that they had with each other. Azziziyah was also the only place where I understood the language spoken around me. It was less isolating, and I had a chance to watch other families exist and compare them to mine.

Even though I had a deep love for the city I considered my hometown, there was a general sense that I was not welcome in Jeddah because of my South Asian heritage. I felt this in the stares and sometimes in the way we were called 'Hindi', the Arabic word for Indian. When we moved to our first expat compound, I was fourteen and mistaken for a childminder. The Asian women, especially from Indonesia and the Philippines, came to Saudi Arabia to be domestic helpers and the local news was peppered with stories of assaults against these women. The working-class immigrant men did not have it any better.

I remember witnessing a car accident in which a Saudi man drove into a South Asian's car when he changed lanes on the roundabout. It was a minor accident and it was the Saudi's fault. Instead of apologising, he stormed out of his car, pulled the South Asian out of his seat and banged the poor man's head repeatedly on the car's doorframe. No one came to his rescue and I did not even wonder why Papa did not stop to help. We all knew our precarious place in this country of plenty. Being immigrants in a place where Asians were treated like second-class citizens was an integral part of my childhood.

This issue was never addressed openly in my family, but it was something I felt acutely. I knew that no matter how many years of their lives my parents spent in Saudi Arabia, they would never be accepted. Yet I was constantly reminded by both my parents to feel grateful to this country for our family's livelihood. I understood that the end goal was to feel like I shouldn't belong, so I never tried. I knew that Jeddah was not long-term, and I was at peace with the fact that my parents would eventually move back to India.

I made my first 'best friend' around this time. Our fathers worked in the same company and we went to the same school. Our mothers got on with each other and Mama approved of my friend because she got good grades and kept a clean room. She was a year ahead of me at school and I looked up to her. We met at social gatherings and shared a love of books. We told each other our secrets and exchanged friendship bracelets. We remained close friends throughout our childhood and manoeuvred through adolescence together. We made fun of our parents' quirks and treated each other's younger siblings like our own. While we discussed everything, we never shared our thoughts on the precarious position we held in our home-town. We were not taught to be nuanced and so we didn't know it was possible to love something and still critique it. The few times in my childhood that I did try to talk to someone about how I felt in Jeddah, I was admonished. My friend's mother once told me that Saudis are the descendants of our Prophet and I should show them more respect.

Along with erratic hours and working at weekends, Papa's work also involved a lot of travelling. Sometimes he would be gone for a few weeks at a stretch. He came home with stories from other Gulf countries, North America, Europe and East Asia. He bought us gifts and told us about how people live in these far-flung countries. His stories fascinated me as much as the Hello Kitty merchandise he brought back for me. I also had an enviable collection of hotel notepads when I was at school and was endlessly showing off the cheap, branded ballpoints to my friends.

While Papa was away on these business trips, the rest of us were usually confined to our home, with the exception of travelling to school. At that time in Saudi Arabia, Mama could not just walk out of the house with her children. This meant that, even though she was a stay-at-home mother for most of my childhood, we hardly ever got to do things with her outside our home. The lack of mobility also meant that I was stuck with my parents' pre-established social circles well into my teen years. In fact, wherever we went, we went as a family unit because my parents were afraid to leave us home alone, in a country that was foreign to them.

At this age, I only cared for trips to the bookshop and even these involved a lot of planning, wheedling and begging. Though reading was encouraged in my family, a lot depended on how busy my parents were that weekend and whether Papa was not too tired to take us to a bookshop and wait while I browsed.

If the trip was finally about to happen, I also had to make sure it was timed well so I did not get to the shop just before it shut for *salah*, the Muslim prayers which took place five times a day. It is mandatory for Muslims to pray five times and it is a rule in Saudi Arabia that all businesses should shut for the duration of each prayer. I guess this was meant to encourage piety, but it just got in the way of my book shopping. When we did go to the bookshop, I was allowed to buy one book at a time. If Papa was away on one of his trips, it meant endless weeks without new books.

There was a well-stocked library at school, but for some reason, the librarian did not allow us to touch the books on the shelves. The shelves were neatly stacked, and the books gleamed behind locked, glass doors. We had a library period squeezed into our weekly schedule but depending on the librarian's mood, we were either allowed to sit quietly and wait for our turn to pick a book from a preassigned shelf or wait in our classroom while our class monitors picked up the preapproved books (usually copies of *Asterix* or *Tintin* comics). The next week at the same hour, we placed these books on the teacher's desk in our classroom. The monitors counted them and took them to the library while the class remained seated, waiting for the next round of books. Sometimes the monitors returned empty-handed, to loud booing.

I did not understand this need to censor and so I harboured many ill feelings towards the librarian. She was a quiet person and lacked distinct personality traits, to my mind. During the ten years I studied at the school, I do not remember once interacting with her. I took her need to protect the books as a personal affront and hated her with all my might.

International Indian School, Jeddah was crowded, with ten sections for each year and an average of fifty students in each section. This meant that there were two libraries for 6000 students, one for primary school and the other for secondary as well as high school. Maybe the sheer number of students made it impossible for each of us to withdraw books every week. There were also no public libraries in Jeddah when I lived there.

Between restricted library access and occasional bookshop visits, I was always in need of a good story. I appreciated the many gifts Papa brought us back from his trips, but it was the stories that I looked forward to, especially the ones about the people he met on his travels. A story that has stayed with me all these years is of an American soldier who sat beside Papa on a flight to the States. He was young, with terrible body odour, and was going home for the first time in two years, after fighting in Iraq. He had flown to Germany first, to meet his girlfriend, who broke up with him immediately. He was wounded in Iraq but didn't want to talk about it. There was no one waiting for him in America either. 'No home, no hope, no job,' Papa said. To return after two years with no one to receive him at the airport was heartbreaking.

Of all the people Papa told me about, it is this soldier that I think about from time to time. I hope he has found love again and I hope people around him remember that he is allergic to cashews.

My early obsession with Mama started to wane. In 1999, five days after my eight birthday, my sister Rasha was born. The birth was a surprise to both Raiyan and me. Soon after Mama came home with her newborn, friends and relatives descended on us with congratulations and best wishes. During one such visit, Papa's colleague's wife asked Mama how it felt to be a mother after six years. I remember sitting beside Mama when she was asked this, and I looked at her, waiting for an answer. I wanted to know how Mama felt. It was a question I had never thought to ask her. But there was no answer. She must have demurred with a smile.

I wonder now what Mama's life must have been like during those early years of motherhood, when Raiyan and I were born. Mama married young and moved to Saudi Arabia to be with Papa and a couple of years later had two children in quick succession. Having been married for a few years myself now, I find it hard to imagine the challenges she must have faced as a newly married woman in a country where she did not speak the local language and did not know anyone except her husband. Not only was she expected to adhere to the strict Saudi rules, she was also expected to live hundreds of miles away from the only home she knew.

When my sister was three, Mama went back to her education. She had a bachelor's degree from a time before her marriage. She topped this up with a degree in Montessori education through distance learning. Her ambition as a young girl was to become a lawyer but living in Saudi Arabia limited her career choices to medicine or teaching. The studies came as a surprise to me, but I do not remember them ever affecting her role as a mother. I do not know how she managed this feat. Though Papa was around, he had not yet started helping with the household chores. That came later.

Mama got her education and waited until my sister was old enough to start school before applying for jobs. My sister's first school was also Mama's first place of work. Mama's move from homemaker to professional marked the beginning of a new era in our family. It also marked the beginning of my teen years.

My relationship with Mama continued to be strained. In contrast, her relationships with my siblings were markedly different, characterised by inside jokes, camaraderie and laughter. But my jokes seemed to fall flat, my efforts appeared condescending. By now, she had told me I couldn't see her happy and it made me wonder if I was the problem after all. I decided to give our relationship another go.

On one of our summer holidays in Sirsi, I noticed how much Mama enjoyed going through her childhood photos. Every year, she went through them but never took any of them with her to Jeddah. I wanted to replicate this joy for her and decided to handcraft a birthday gift for her. Without her knowledge, I took some of her precious photos and hid them in my backpack. When we returned to Jeddah I laboured over a collage for her for months, carefully framing her pictures and decorating the spaces in between. I sourced household items and spent my pocket money on decorations. I mounted the pictures on cardboard and decorated it for days, after school and between homework and Qur'an classes.

Finally, the day arrived. I waited for her to come back from school. She came in flustered, as usual, and got annoyed with me for not clearing up the dining table. I wished her happy birthday, but she didn't respond. She was already rummaging in the kitchen to start making the next meal. I probably did not choose my moment intelligently, but I was too excited to wait any longer. I slipped into my room and came out with my collage. 'Mama, look,' I said. I lifted the collage in front of my face and missed her expression. There was sudden silence, no sounds of her moving things about in the kitchen. I had left her awestruck, I thought. I was expecting a hug, a thank you, at the very least. When I put the collage down, instead of happiness, I saw anger. She launched into a tirade I couldn't understand. This was not how it was supposed to go. She was angry with me for taking her photos. For bringing them to Jeddah, for putting them on cardboard, for ruining her memories. I could not believe what was happening; I started crying. Mama said many things but the words that remain are how I'm always ruining the little happiness she has in life.

I slid the collage back under my bed and tried to forget about the incident. When my own anger failed to subside, I pulled the collage from its hiding place and ripped it to shreds and threw it in the bin. Mama never asked to see it again and I never had to explain to her that her precious pictures were no more.

Living in Saudi Arabia had become a way of life for me and I rarely compared its restrictions to the relative freedom women enjoyed in India. The rules have relaxed now but from the 1970s to the 2000s, Saudi Arabia was still policing women's bodies in the name of Islam.

The country had strict moral policing when Mama first moved to Saudi Arabia. Both my parents maintain that this was a happy time in their lives and that they enjoyed these early years together. Both seem unfazed by the framework of gender inequality within which they began their married life. However, I often wonder about the impact these restrictions had on Mama. How does a woman go from wearing beautiful blue dresses to a black uniform? How does one make peace with being invisible in a crowd?

Though I never witnessed any of this violence myself, women of Mama's generation were full of stories about public lashings of women by the moral police for showing their ankles. The police sometimes threw red dye on the women they felt were 'shamefully dressed', which usually translated as 'having an uncovered face or head'. In my time, the moral police still walked with an entourage in malls and other public spaces and verbally reprimanded women, but there was no punishment.

At school and at home, I was taught that bad things happen to girls who are not 'good Muslims'. Every week in school, we had an Islamic class in which we studied chapters from the Qur'an and how to pray. The Islamic teacher narrated stories from the Prophet's life and asked questions based on these stories. The teacher also taught us the importance of wearing the hijab and explained that our duties as good Muslim women included being good mothers and obedient wives. From a young age, I had a conflicted relationship with the hijab and while most of my friends wore the scarf once they hit puberty, I resisted.

These 'Islamic' lessons were not limited to the Islamic class. Other subject teachers also took liberties in talking to us about our duties as Muslim girls and how we should take pride in being Muslims because it was the first religion to give women their rights. Both my parents and my teachers asserted that men and women are considered equal in the eyes of Allah. This went against my lived experiences and I challenged it often. Papa was most vocal about these so-called rights. He would compare the status of Muslim women to those of the women in the West. He spoke about how they weren't even allowed to vote until the last century while Muslim women have held these rights – to vote, own property, keep their name after marriage, accept dowry and, if necessary, divorce their husbands – for over 1400 years. When I questioned why men created obstacles for women to access these rights, I was told that men and women are equal but not 'identical', that men knew better.

A popular verse from the Qur'an was often quoted at me when I questioned the inequality of men and women. It roughly translates as 'women can't be inherited against their will and should be treated with kindness'. This verse was meant to highlight the magnanimity of Muslim men. But the verse comes with a caveat ('except when they have been guilty of open lewdness') which is often used against women. The description of 'lewdness' can change with circumstances to include everything from 'promiscuity' to disobedience towards parents.

I was not convinced about the respectful place women supposedly held in Islam and my insistence on approaching this subject with logic often annoyed my elders. I was reminded that questioning the will of Allah is a sin. When I countered that I'm questioning the will of man, not Allah, I was asked to increase my knowledge and stop speaking from a place of ignorance. My questioning was considered a kind of lewdness.

There was one PE teacher who kept us in class from time to time to lecture us on the importance of keeping our bodies safe from any unwanted touch and gaze. She was also the only person, during my childhood, who spoke about the rampant groping that was going on in public spaces in Jeddah. This was not a topic I discussed with friends or family and I was not sure how many others were experiencing it. This class was the only place where this subject was ever addressed. The teacher spoke, and we listened in silence, careful not to make eye contact with each other.

I remember the teacher telling us about a man who grabbed

her from behind while she was shopping with her husband. I assumed this was going to be another lesson on staying close to your family and being aware of yourself in public spaces. Instead, she told us about how she turned around and slapped the man across his face.

A couple of years before this, I was groped in the same market that my teacher was talking about. I was in a shoe shop with my family to buy new shoes for my brother when I realised that a man was following me. I took a few abrupt turns to confirm this suspicion and started looking for my parents. In my confusion, I forgot to maintain my distance from the man and immediately, I felt a hand on my bottom. I do not remember how long this lasted but the next thing I remember is Mama screaming at the man as he shuffled out of the shop. She asked Papa to do something and continued to shout in the general direction of the door through which the man had escaped. She looked weary. Papa did not follow the man.

Mama turned to me and scolded me for not staying in her line of sight like she had asked me to. Just before she turned away, she yanked the lollipop out of my mouth and told me to stop attracting unwanted attention. I held a hand to my cheek, trying not whimper from the pain of hard candy cracking against my teeth. I was eleven.

Papa once told me that according to Islam, a woman will be 500 years away from heaven each time a *ghayr mahram* (unrelated) man touches her. 'How many years away will the man be from heaven for touching her?' I asked. My father did not know.

The Qur'an teachers who came to our home each weekday after school were also keen to make sure that I understood my place in our society. Over the years, we had a string of Qur'an teachers visiting us. We called them *maulanas*. One *maulana* liked to talk about women's bodies and the changes we went through at puberty in detail while watching me squirm. He seemed to take pleasure in making me uncomfortable and all I could do was fix my gaze on his smirk. These men were so revered by my parents; I did not quite know how to explain to them about what was happening.

If the men of religion were beyond reproach, so was the patriarchal structure. We were not to question this. Because of the expectations placed on mothers to police their daughters, any dissent was considered a personal insult to their mothering. A lot went unsaid between mothers and daughters because of this shared fear. While I yearned for a carefree childhood and unconditional love, Mama needed me to be in touch with the reality of being a young woman in my community. My innocence was not celebrated; it was a point of contention. My inability to imbibe the pressures I should be feeling as a young girl in my community made Mama's role within the patriarchy that much more difficult.

In turn, I felt that Mama held my joyful hope against me. I wanted a mother who could see me for who I was and not worry about how I would be perceived by our society. This 'thing' became an invisible fence that kept us both distant from each other during my growing years. At the time, I did not have the language nor the understanding to cross this fence. We remained unable to free ourselves of the restrictions placed on us by the patriarchy, even when it threatened to create an insurmountable barrier between us.

When I stepped out of the house in my adolescent years, I feared being caught out by the *mutawas* (moral police). I learned at a young age to stay alert and to avert my eyes when they cornered their target. A hush would fall in their presence and people spoke in whispers. The *mutawas* wore traditional white *thobes* (robes) and a *ghutrah* (headcloth) kept in place with an *agal*, a heavy black cord. Over their *thobes* they wore a black or dark-coloured *bisht*, a cloak which is often worn over a *thobe*. The *bisht* distinguished them from other men. Their entourage of policemen also helped us spot the *mutawas* from a distance. They came to mind when I watched the French police make a Muslim woman disrobe on a beach in 2016. It was jarring to see a scene from my childhood play out on a European beach.

The Handmaid's Tale makes for good TV, but for me it was a lived reality. An episode in which Moira, one of the handmaids, makes a bold attempt to escape the Red Center (a place where women are held against their wishes and forced into surrogacy), reminded me of Dina Ali Lasloom, a twenty-four-year-old Saudi woman who was on her way to seek asylum in Australia. During a stopover in Manila, airport officials reported her to their Saudi counterparts and detained her in a hotel room until her family claimed her. When June, another handmaid, was punished for attempting to escape, I wondered what Lasloom's home-coming was like.

I followed Lasloom's story closely when it broke, and one detail has always stayed with me. A security official witnessed men assumed to be Lasloom's relatives carry her out of the hotel room with duct tape on her mouth, feet and hands. The official saw her struggle to break free before she was placed in a wheelchair and taken to the plane that would fly her back to Saudi Arabia.

In the introduction to the 2017 edition of *The Handmaid's Tale*, Margaret Atwood reiterates that every horror mentioned in the book has happened in some part of the world. The book was published in 1985, thirty-two years before Dina's failed attempt to escape her abusers.

*   *   *

From teachers, friends, family and the moral police, the message was clear: the world was a dangerous place for women and we needed to be careful at all times.

Mama was the first person to tell me about rape. I was ten and Mama was in my room to tuck me in with a bedtime story. I was not sure why she was telling me the story about a girl who agreed to meet a boy from her school. The girl did not inform her parents where she was going and took a girl-friend with her. The boy asked them to come to a hotel and took them both to a room upstairs. Once they were inside, he locked the door and several boys jumped out of the ward-robes and raped them. She ended this story with, 'be careful'. When I nodded, she insisted, 'promise me'.

The word 'rape' did not mean anything to me then. The story confused me more than it scared me. I do not think Mama used the word 'jump' but that is how I imagined the boys springing out of the wardrobes. I thought that was the scary bit, boys jumping out of wardrobes.

These stories continued to find me throughout my child-hood. Sometimes friends phoned up to tell me something they overheard their mothers talking about. Once a friend told me about a girl from our school who was kidnapped right outside our school building and gang-raped by a group of men in a car parked not far from where she was picked up. By this point I had figured out the full significance of this act and was devastated. However, my friend was not done with her story. When the last man got in the car for his turn, he found out that it was his sister. For days, I agonised over this last detail. How a woman in my city was possibly living in the same house as a man who was partly responsible for her assault.

I was six when I was groped for the first time. I was at a family friend's house and the man was their help, the one who usually took charge of the children. The children were playing in the basement while the adults had dinner upstairs. He initiated a game of catch and ran after me. He grabbed me in a way that at first felt normal but then became painful. His palms pressed hard on my flat chest. I lost my enthusiasm and managed to disengage from the game. I tried going upstairs to Mama but was promptly sent back.

The man continued working with that family for many years. When I was twelve and back in that house to celebrate their child's birthday, he came up behind my best friend, grabbed her bottom and brushed his body against hers with the pretext of serving her dinner. My friend confronted him immediately, putting her plate down and turning to face him. I was standing beside her and turned too but wasn't sure what was happening. When I asked, she looked the man in the eyes and said, 'Do you want to tell her or shall I?' He smiled sheepishly and left the kitchen. My friend explained what he had done.

A few months later, they hosted another party and both my family and my friend's family were invited. My friend and I stayed close to each other and avoided being around the man. The children were in the TV room and the hostess, whom we called Auntie, came to check that we were eating. She saw that my friend's plate was empty and asked her to go to the dining room and help herself to more food. When my friend stood up, I stood up too. This action on my part provoked Auntie and she scolded us for being glued together all the time. I did not understand what was happening and remained silent. Auntie then scolded my friend in front of the other children for spreading lies and thinking too highly of herself. We were the eldest in the group and the children looked on, unsure. Some went back to watching TV, some continued eating as though nothing was happening. My friend left the room. I sat back down and watched as Auntie shut the door behind her.

My friend returned a few minutes later and put a slice of pizza on my plate. We nibbled in silence and when I was sure no one was paying any attention, I asked her what Auntie meant. Apparently, when they returned home from the birthday party all those months ago, she told her mother about what the man had done.

'What did your mother do?' I asked.

'She told me it was okay, that I was right to come to her. Then she called Auntie.'

'Then what happened?'

We were whispering.

'Nothing. She heard what my mother had to say and then she hung up.'

'I don't think it was right of her to shout at you like that.'

'I know.'

'Sorry I didn't say anything.'

'There is nothing to say.'

The truth is that there was something to say but I chose not to. I could have told my friend that this happened to me too, by the same man, six years ago. But having just witnessed my friend being humiliated in front of our peers for speaking up made me never want to share my own story with anyone, not even her. I was not even a teenager yet and my culture had already taught me how to remain silent in the face of such violations of women's bodies.

I never questioned these rules and the expectations placed on women and girls to uphold the patriarchal value system. Saudi culture was the only culture I knew and a part of me did assume that this was how all Muslim communities functioned. The year I turned thirteen, Papa planned a family holiday to the UK. We were visiting his brother, my uncle, and would split our time between London and Newcastle. I was fascinated by London, and it was the first place where I felt like I was part of the crowd. I was an extremely self-conscious child and it was liberating to walk on the streets of London and not be subject to second glances. The city's nonchalance towards me felt like acceptance, permission even. Maybe I could be who I wanted to be after all. This experience stuck with me and over the years, I thought of it whenever I imagined my future.

In Saudi Arabia I was both invisible and hyper-visible. Some men went about their day as though I did not exist in public spaces while some made the experience of existing in such spaces uncomfortable. In London, I existed without either of these feelings being shoved down my throat. And I wondered if I could experience that again.

This trip to London also exposed me to something else. One of Papa's business associates invited our family for dinner at his place. They were a Muslim family of Iranian origin and I was stunned by the way things worked in their household. His wife was an integral part of the dinner conversation and we all sat together to eat. Papa's friend often turned to his wife for confirmation of the anecdotes he was sharing, and I loved how they both helped set the table and bring the food out. It was a far cry from the social gatherings I was used to attending and it left a deep impression on me. It showed me that a different life was possible.

A year after Mama began working, she noticed that my hair was thinning. This was not cause for major concern because I had thick hair. So thick, in fact, that throughout my childhood I had a 'bob' cut as this was the only way to manage my hair. Mama decided that oiling my hair regularly was the answer. With three children to manage and a full-time job, her time was precious. Yet she found time to oil my hair, comb through it carefully and read long *duas* (Islamic prayers) and blow over my head, according to tradition. When the thinning continued, Mama turned first to Ayurveda and then to homeopathy. It was only when I turned fourteen that the real panic set in.

The yearly trips to India which used to be filled with care-free time spent at my grandparents' homes were now spent scouting for new doctors and hoping they could figure out what was wrong with me. Tests were ordered, and results read with hand under chin. Many of these visits were peppered with my parents getting their hopes up. Occasionally, I allowed myself to feel hopeful too. I clearly remember Mama's reactions when a doctor spoke for the first time after examining me. Often close to tears, she would wring her hands. Her forehead would crease, her eyes round, and she would lean forward. When she asked, 'But why, Doctor?' I think what she really wanted to ask was, 'But why me, Doctor?'

While the doctor coughed and also leaned forward, trying to think of the best way to respond, I did not know who I felt sorrier for, the doctor or my mother. In those early years of hair loss, I never felt sorry for myself. I had my tricks to hide the thinning and it was not getting in the way of my lifestyle.

This seemed to bother my parents. Once, on a second visit to a doctor in India, he asked me if I was still taking the tablets he had prescribed the year before. I said, 'No, I stopped taking them,' having given up after six months. The doctor had promised results within three months but there was no change even after six. Also, I was a lazy child. The doctor slammed his desk with glee. 'See, this is why it did not work!' he told my parents. 'There is nothing wrong with my medicine, next time make sure your daughter is actually taking it.' He seemed relieved to find a loophole, to be able to shift the blame. Mama was aghast, Papa angry, and Dadi, my paternal grandmother, who accompanied us on these visits to the doctor's, sat in silence.

No one said anything when we stepped out of the clinic. Papa phoned the driver and we waited for him to pull over. I got in the back and sat between Mama and Dadi. Papa sat in the passenger seat and asked the driver to take us home. That did not sound right. Papa had promised that we would go to the mall after the doctor's visit to buy me a new pair of jeans. When I reminded Papa of his promise, he scolded me for being irresponsible. He said I did not care about the money they were spending, the time this was taking and the consequences of my inactions.

I stayed quiet. Deep down I knew that hair did not just grow back. Once you start balding, you are balding, end of story. I watched the driver in the rear-view mirror, embarrassed to be scolded in front of him. There was silence for a while and then Dadi turned to Mama and said she should be doing a better job of raising her children and should have known that I was not taking my medicine. No one spoke up in Mama's defence and when I tried to say something, Mama snapped at me to keep quiet. In the silence that followed, I could hear Mama sniffling beside me.

If I had been allowed to speak, I would have told Dadi about how during one round of homeopathy medication, Mama woke up a couple of hours before everyone else, came to my room in the dark (so as not to disturb my sister with whom I shared a room at the time), made me sit up in my sleep and forced a small cap of tiny round pills into my mouth. The doctor's instructions were clear: place the pills under one's tongue and let them dissolve. No chewing or hurried swallowing. It was important that I ate nothing for an hour after I took the sweet pills. Brushing my teeth was not allowed either. Many mornings I would wake up with the pills still undissolved in my mouth, swallow them quickly, and go and brush my teeth.

If I had been allowed to speak, I would have told Dadi about all the *duas* Mama read and the amount of time she spent every day reading certain pages from the Qur'an for her children's safety, happiness and success. How she watched over us, cried when we got hurt, made sure we were eating a balanced diet, and sat with us each evening to ensure we completed our homework, on top of her full-time job. I did not know what else Mama could have done to be a better mother. I don't know what hurt most, Dadi's words or Papa's silence.

My hair loss worsened at the peak of my teenage years and I could no longer pretend it away. I had to confront my reality. While I was still figuring out ways to come to terms with what was happening, I also found myself consoling Mama whenever she burst into tears at the sight of me studying, walking, reading or talking. Anything could set her off when we were home and I started avoiding being around her. When it could not be avoided, I patted her hand and listened as she told me about how the knowledge of my hair loss would wake her up in the middle of the night and leave a sharp, stabbing pain in her stomach. I was not always sure how to respond when she lamented my fate and looked at me with pity.

Though conversation was always halting with my mother, things became dire during my teenage years. While most teenage daughters seem to have a difficult relationship with their mothers, mine was further strained by my hair loss. I felt that Mama needed me to worry about it every waking moment of my life. My hair loss meant different things to us both, but we did not have the words to communicate our fears to each other. And when we did, they came out in angry bursts.

Mama became pedantic about medication and began monitoring my habits to ensure that my scalp was getting enough nutrition and blood circulation. Around this time, a group of classmates planned a trip to an amusement park. I could not commit until I had permission from my parents. That evening, I went to Mama's bedroom to ask. She was sitting on the bed with an array of papers and books around her, making a lesson plan for her students.

The moment I stepped in, she glanced in my direction and back to her papers.

'Have you done your exercise today?' she asked.

I had not.

'Do it here, now,' she responded.

Exercise is the wrong word for what she was asking me to do. One of the Indian doctors had mentioned that our scalps do not get enough blood and that I should spend up to fifteen minutes with my head in a position lower than the rest of my body. She suggested that I lie on a bed with my head hanging from the edge. I moved Mama's papers to make space for myself on the bed. I held my position and stared at the ceiling. My mind wandered. When I thought I had done my time, I lifted my head and said, 'So some of my friends are going to the amusement park.'

This was a wrong move. Apparently, Mama was keeping an eye on the clock and I had not stayed in my position at the edge of the bed for the exact time that was required. Mama screamed at me and in her anger and frustration, she said something about how my hair was more important than my desire to traipse around town with my friends.

I took this literally and believed that Mama needed me to stay home and lament my hair loss every single waking hour. I believed that Mama could not tolerate my happiness and that she needed a companion in mourning my losses. Thus began my journey into womanhood.

There were other sensitive subjects too. At school, girls were getting periods, which made me curious. I usually went to Papa when I had questions, but I gathered that this was something that needed to be between women. I found my moment when we were out shopping as a family. My siblings went with Papa and I followed Mama to the women's clothes section.

'Mama, what are periods?' I asked.

I could sense her discomfort and it made me uncomfortable too.

'It is when women bleed,' she said.

'Where do they bleed from?' I asked.

'From their private parts,' she responded.

'Does it hurt?' I asked.

'Stop asking so many questions and go and find Papa,' she said.

I sensed anger. I felt dirty. I wish I had not brought it up. By asking, I felt as though I had admitted vulnerability. I did not want Mama to think she knew things that I did not.

When I did finally get my period, Mama did not speak to me about it. Papa was travelling and when he returned, he sat at the other end of the dining table from me and asked me how I was feeling. I was up late, revising for a test. Everyone else in the house was asleep. 'I feel okay,' I replied, unsure what he was referring to. Before I could ask him to clarify, he alluded to this change in me. The word mature was used. I sat motionless long after he left the table and walked slowly to my bedroom, uncomfortable in my new role as a mature girl.

When my hair loss started to show, I worried about my classmates noticing. I cried when I was alone and every morning I avoided meeting my gaze in the mirror. I did not tell my parents about the debilitating fear I felt every time I entered the school building.

My hair loss soon became difficult to hide; none of my comb-over options worked. I figured I could fill the visible spots in my jet-black hair with kohl as camouflage. I did not wear any makeup but to validate my request to own kohl pencils, I wore some around my eyes. It was going to be my secret – I was always careful to wash it off before a doctor's appointment.

One day during yet another summer break in India, I was caught off-guard. Mama wanted to go shopping and asked if I would accompany her. I made sure we could stop at a bookshop before getting in the car with her. It just so happened that the bookshop I wanted to go to was close to a doctor we had seen the year before, a doctor whom I did not trust at all. Something about him made me shudder. I did not have any excuse and before I knew it, we were in the waiting room with a walk-in appointment. I considered sneaking into the toilet and washing off the kohl streaks. But that would leave my baldness visible and I did not have a bandana with me. Also, there was a risk of getting my hair wet and how was I going to explain that? I sat on my hands and tried not to panic.

When it was our turn, I walked in behind Mama. The doctor and Mama exchanged pleasantries, the doctor asked how I was doing and then he sat me down and examined my scalp. I closed my eyes.

'Are you wearing any cover up?' he asked.

I opened my eyes and saw Mama lean in, her eyes round, her lips quivering.

'Yes,' I answered.

Mama had not comprehended it yet. The doctor was laughing. I closed my eyes again.

Now Mama asked me the same question.

'Yes, I comb my hair and after pinning it, I colour in the visible scalp,' I said.

Mama looked as if someone had punched her. This meant that my hair loss was even worse than she imagined.

'It's okay,' the doctor told Mama. Maybe this doctor is not that bad after all, I thought.

He pulled off his gloves, threw them in the bin and sat back in his chair. Mama asked him a series of questions about the kohl and if it would damage my scalp. He listened patiently, shook his head and confirmed that it was okay to use the kohl.

He then proceeded to ask Mama if she had heard of the new laser comb. Mama was all ears. He talked at length about the features, how it would help blood circulation in the scalp and regenerate new hair and strengthen old hair, and before I knew it Mama was buying me an overpriced gadget. I was to comb my hair with it for fifteen minutes twice a day. Just as we were leaving his office, he stopped us and said, 'Since you are going to start using the laser comb, you should not use any cover up.'

My heart sank. I was not allowed to wear a bandana at school and some of the girls I knew could be cruel. I knew that once the doctor said I could not use cover up, Mama was going to be militant about it. She needed my hair to grow back, but she was not thinking about the impact hair loss was starting to have on my psyche. I did not have the words to explain this to her. When we got into the car, she asked if I wanted to go to the bookshop. I said I wanted to go home and pretended to fall asleep during the car ride back so I did not have to listen to her go on about laser combs.

I know Mama worried about me and I understood that this worry came from a place of good intentions. She treated my hair loss as a sign that she had failed as a parent. With every passing year, it became her biggest issue and I did not know how to reclaim it. She was concerned about what others would say when they found out. This meant that I needed to hide it from almost everyone except my parents and my siblings. This was hard work. If we had unexpected visitors, I would run to my room and shut the door and frantically look for my trusted bandana.

In India, it was even more difficult to hide. Unlike our Jeddah home, we had more visitors and what was once a happy place with lots of people soon became a place in which I needed to keep my guard up.

A few days after Mama asked me to stop using kohl, Dadi received a call from her niece. She wanted to visit us that afternoon. I wanted to cry. I had had a few run-ins with this woman, and none were pleasant. My extended family had an inkling about my hair loss and tried to bring it up every chance they got. They probably did this because of how sad and uncomfortable it made Mama. Without the kohl, my baldness was visible. A bandana would only raise more questions. In any case, the last time I had met this woman, she had tried to pull it off my head. I sat still in the living room downstairs. From the kitchen, I could hear Dadi telling the maids to prepare tea and to expect guests. From where I was sitting, I saw Mama in the kitchen with the maids and I knew exactly what she was thinking.

After a long while, she walked over and sat down beside me and said, 'Your auntie is visiting, do you want to use the kohl as cover up?' I could not believe it. I jumped up from the couch and ran upstairs to find my kohl pencil just as the doorbell rang. Mama stayed downstairs to greet the woman and her daughters. I did the best I could and went downstairs too. As soon as I entered the kitchen, and as if on cue, the woman said, 'Oh Zeba, your hair looks nice.' She then turned to Mama and said, 'Her hair is looking nice.' Mama nodded politely and went back to serving tea. The woman looked at me again and smirked.

I wonder if things would have been easier if I could have

been open about my imperfections. Would they stop caring once they realised that we did not care? That it did not bother Mama, that there was nothing new to see here? Interactions like this kept repeating themselves during every visit to India. The culprits were always Papa's side of the family. I think his aversion to confrontations and his need to maintain a united family gave his relatives permission to behave as they liked.

When that woman's daughter was diagnosed with a serious neurological condition and she wanted to keep it a secret, I was shocked by my desire to call her up and ask her about it. I wanted to rub it in her face. I wanted to hurt her the way she hurt me, I wanted to smirk the way she did, I wanted to say, 'Oh no, look at your daughter's beautiful hair which will be shaved for surgery.' Instead, I prayed for her daughter and I prayed for my own morality.

On our next trip to India, the laser comb doctor suggested injecting steroids into my scalp. I remember feeling scared; I hated injections, and getting multiple injections into my scalp was a truly terrifying idea. I sat there, watching him, thinking about his numerous strange and usually under-researched ideas. The doctor introduced the treatment as something new that had neither been tried in the region before, nor ever been done by him. This did not fill me with confidence.

At first I was not worried, because I knew my parents would never consider it. Six injections straight into the scalp. Surely not? Wrong. I was amazed to see my parents make this decision for me. I couldn't believe they didn't ask me what I thought – I was sitting right there. I watched in silence as the doctor stood up, unlocked the cupboard behind his desk and pulled out a box of syringes. I did not tell my parents that I did not want it; I did not have the words.

The doctor asked me to stand up, so he could move my chair into a position that made it possible for him to reach my head. Papa stood beside my chair. When he reached to hold my hand, I let him. I tried not to show my pain, but it was difficult to stay quiet as each jab to my scalp added to my agony.

It was the most painful thing I had experienced. I could not stop thinking about my brain. What if the doctor made a mistake? What if the syringe went too deep? What if I was left with serious injuries? I wished I had had time to ask questions, to be assured that what was being done to me was a safe procedure. I know now that when correctly done, it should not hurt much.

Mama was there too, standing beside Papa, her face wrinkled with worry, her hand on my shoulder flinching with each jab, as though she was being pierced too. When I stood up to leave the doctor's room, I felt dizzy. Mama and Papa held me on either side and walked me to the car. My sister was in the waiting room and when she saw me, she didn't ask any questions, just walked in line behind us.

I do not know if anything was said afterwards, but I remember the silence in the car. My sister tried to make conversation on the drive home but when she saw me biting my lip to hold back my tears she looked away and remained silent too. I remember the pain jolting through my body at every speed bump. I couldn't eat anything when I got home and requested to skip dinner. It was only seven but the thought of enduring the evening was unbearable. I took the prescribed painkillers, excused myself and went to bed.

In bed, I could hear my cousins playing in the adjacent room and I felt relieved that once I was in my room I no longer had to pretend to be okay. I cried into my pillow and was careful not to make a noise. My sister joined me a few hours later and quietly took her place beside me on the double bed we were sharing that summer.

When the house was silent and all the lights were switched off, Mama came to check on me. I pretended to be asleep.

Mama placed her hand on my head and cried. I could feel her tears on my cheek. She stayed like this for a while, in the dark, as though healing from the trauma of that day. I let her. She tucked me in and left the room, closing the door behind her. In the silence she left behind, my sister turned over and whispered, '*Didi*? Are you okay?' I ignored her, shutting my eyes tight and praying that I did not let slip a whimper as I continued to cry.

I finally gave in and wore a headscarf to school, even though I did not like wearing it and was worried that people would think it was a hijab. Knowing that the hijab was a personal and conscious choice made by Muslim women of faith, I felt like a fraud. I felt like my intentions were bad and that by wearing a scarf I was being disrespectful towards women who wear a hijab. By covering my head in order to hide my hair loss, I thought I was sinning, a reaction driven by the unnecessary guilt surrounding modesty in my community.

Because it was sudden and without preamble, many of my friends wanted to know why. I did not want to talk about my hair just yet, so I lied. And that hurt too, because I knew I was better than that.

Meanwhile, it was making me anxious to imagine what would happen if my best friend found out about my hair. In my bid to avoid this, I had made excuses not to have sleepovers with her. I also avoided hugging her and would flinch whenever she surprised me. I couldn't continue like this. When the new school year began, I decided I was going to tell her about my hair.

I sought her out during a lunch break. It was an hour in which we were mostly left to do as we pleased. We walked to the auditorium together and I told her I needed to speak with her. She did not betray any emotions and sat on the stage beside me, our legs dangling off the edge. In front of us, our classmates had scattered, some playing catch, others badminton, some sat in a circle, giggling and gossiping. I told her, 'I have a hair problem.' She wanted to know what this meant. 'I'm losing my hair,' I said. 'Okay,' she responded. We turned to look at each other, silent. Then she smacked me on the back so hard I screamed in pain. 'You're it,' she said, as she slid off the stage and ran into the crowd. I wanted to cry. Both from the physical pain and the emotional exhaustion of trying to find the language to share my secret with my best friend. I remember going to the toilets after and crying, then crying in bed that night. My friend and I never talked about my hair loss again. We are friends to this day.

I did not share these incidents with my parents. There was no language for this pain, there was only space for my mother's tears and trauma about my hair. I had to be the strong one, I could not add to her mounting worries, and her biggest worry of all was my future within our community. I think she felt that my marriageability would decrease considerably because of my thinning hair. She worried about this constantly and was vocal about her fears, completely blind to how her words made me feel, as I was reduced to my marriage prospects and objectified.

Though we never spoke about this directly, she shared these fears with her friends. This annoyed me because I felt like my hair loss was a personal issue and I didn't want others weighing in. Sometimes she would come home with anecdotes of how some woman or other got married despite her baldness and how someone's hair grew back in abundance after she had a baby. This story pleased my mother the most and she repeated it often. She told me how this girl's family tried everything, but nothing worked. On her wedding day she was wearing a wig, Mama informed me. But then she had a baby and all her hair grew back miraculously.

This story did not have the same effect on me as it had on my mother. At fourteen, I did not care for marriage and I was not sure I wanted children. I was not going to give birth based on the false promise of my hair growing back, that much I knew for sure. But for Mama, this was perfect. Not only would I be married and a mother, but out of this I would also get my hair back. Now all we needed was a prospective husband who would marry a girl with thinning hair.

Body positivity can be a challenge at the best of times, but for me it was even more difficult because of Mama's constant worrying at home and the country's continued moral policing outside of the home. School was a safe space, but not for long. While Mama was worried about who would marry me, my friends' mothers were taking proactive steps to ensure that when the time was right, their daughters would have the advantage of beauty on their side. This was starting to rub off on my friends and their language was changing to make space for these expectations. We went from discussing Harry Potter and the Olsen twins to discussing the benefits of home-made facemasks and the importance of finding a good husband. They seemed at ease with this transition. If anyone else was experiencing the same dissonance I was, they did not voice it. Neither did I.

A home-made mask could not fix my hair loss, my issues were deeper than that. While my peers aspired to beauty, I needed to approach it differently. I think there are two ways to exist with beauty, especially as teenage girls. You are either engulfed within it or grappling without. My hair loss positioned me on the outskirts of beauty. This saved me from the default path of aspiring to be beautiful. The hair loss meant I knew I couldn't be attractive in a way that was considered acceptable. This knowledge pushed me off the conventional path early on and I was left on the sidelines trying to find my way to a place where how I looked was not intrinsic to my self-esteem.

I knew I could not go on living with this feeling of not being enough. It was important for me to focus on what I had rather than to measure my self-worth against what was missing. With every passing year, I was losing more hair and with it, my chance at a conventional future within my community. Beauty is an essential tool for women within the patriarchy. In strict patriarchal structures, beauty also means options. Sometimes these options could mean a wider pool of potential husbands to choose from and a chance to improve your socio-economic status by marrying up. Because of the way patriarchal communities react to beauty (with kindness and awe), it also means gentler treatment from people around you. But beauty is the illusion of power and choice. Nobody's beauty has served them beyond their marriage. As they say in my community, once you are married, it's the same pots and pans for all women. However short-lived this power, I did not have it and I did not like how that felt.

During my time in Jeddah, I remember being complimented twice for how I looked. Once by Mama, on one of the rare occasions when her staring at me did not end with her in tears. I caught her gaze and instead of looking away she said, 'Wow Zeba, you are so beautiful, such a sharp jawline and straight nose.' The surprise in her voice stung as deep as her tears.

The second time also involved a mother, but not mine. I was at a friend's house after our last A Level exam. It was a farewell party of sorts, and my whole class was there. Her mother was fussing over us, making sure we were eating. When she came to check on me, she looked me in the eye and said, 'You are so beautiful, your face lights up when you smile.' She patted my head and went into the adjacent room to check on others. That moment was the highlight of my last year in Jeddah.

By emphasising beauty, the patriarchy has created a structure in which women are forced to focus on superficial aspects. Judging a gender by their looks can only foster insecurities and that is the intention. School friends who had known each other since kindergarten grew distant because their experiences of the patriarchy were no longer the same.

I was about to turn sixteen and had to figure out a way to accept myself in an environment that was keen to strip me of all my self-worth. There was no doubting the fact that, because of my hair loss, I was not conventionally beautiful. Without beauty, how was I going to navigate my life? Instead of seeking approval from the society I lived in, I decided to observe its response to beauty.

At home, within the community and at school, I recorded the reactions, tones and impressions inspired by beauty. It helped me gauge people and decide if I wanted to be associated with them. Teachers favoured conventionally beautiful girls and praised them openly. One of our teachers was known to be on the lookout for brides for her two young sons. I realised this was not a rumour the day she stopped my friend in the school hallway to ask her age. It was too random to be about anything else.

You can tell a lot about someone by the way they respond to beauty. Is their first reaction admiration or envy? Do they even notice beauty? Do they accept it or reject it? Do they crave it beyond all reason? I was with my friend when the teacher stopped her to ask her age. The teacher did not ask my age. In fact, she did not even look at me while I stood beside my friend and watched them slide into easy conversation and laughter.

By distancing my self-worth from my body, I was distancing myself from the harshness that surrounded unconventional looks and the bitterness that can come from being rejected. This distancing gave me the space I needed to become myself.

I reasoned that the only way to protect my heart and to take the sting out of the harsh words was to find another way to measure myself. I discarded makeup (I still struggle with it) and picked up books, the heavier the better.

Observing other people's reactions towards beauty helped me work on my own feelings towards it. Envy can be a natural response to beauty and I learned to curb it. Instead, I taught myself how to appreciate beauty and not feel threatened by it. This was the first of many lessons that I needed to teach myself in order to survive within the patriarchy.

My self-confidence and my nonchalance towards beauty threatened people around me. My friends' mothers struggled to make sense of it and worried that my confidence might rub off on their own daughters. I sensed their uneasiness and did not know how to placate them.

My decision to distance myself from conventional aspirations left me feeling alienated from my community. Even my own mother couldn't understand how I was going to survive. Mama has always been conventionally beautiful and she was used to people responding to it. At parties, everyone commented on how beautiful Mama looked. Girls my age were also enamoured by her.

Once, I was stopped in the school corridor by an older girl who wanted to know my mother's makeup routine. She was at a party we went to over the weekend. But before she asked me the question, she asked me to confirm that I was my mother's daughter. 'You look nothing like her,' she mused. This wasn't the first time someone had said that. Even if they only meant that I looked different, I couldn't help but take it as a criticism. The girl wanted to know the name of the rouge Mama used. I didn't have the answer but promised to check with Mama. That evening, when Mama was preparing dinner, I broached the subject. I had never shown interest in her makeup before and the question surprised her.

'Where did you get your rouge from?'

'How do you know what rouge is?'

'I know it's the red colour on your cheeks.'

'It's natural.'

'Please tell me the name.' I was already getting impatient.

Mama sighed. It seemed I was not the first person to ask this question.

'I'm telling the truth, come and look.'

Sure enough, the red on her cheeks was natural.

'How did you get such rosy cheeks?'

'I ate lots of tomatoes.'

Now it was my turn to sigh. Mama smiled and said, 'When I was little someone told me I would have beautiful rosy cheeks if I ate lots of tomatoes, so every day I would eat raw tomatoes.' I realised Mama was speaking the truth. I could tell, too, that she was pleased someone had noticed it. But I worried that this answer would make me sound like a liar in front of the older girl and her friends. I decided to give her the name of a generic makeup brand if she asked me again.

During the years I lived in Jeddah, we were constantly moving house. Eventually we moved to an expat compound where my parents still live today. Such compounds were full of amenities not accessible to those living in flats and were popular among Western expats. This final compound was a big space with over 1000 bungalows enclosed by compound walls tens of metres high. Each bungalow had its own wall and independent gate. Every guest was checked in at the main entrance and not let in without the permission of the resident they were visiting. These measures were in place to prevent a copycat attack that shook Saudi Arabia in 2003, when three compounds in Riyadh were bombed by Saudi extremists who were against the westernisation of their country.

When I lived in Jeddah, the compound had three leisure centres fitted with swimming pools, cafés, tennis courts, snooker rooms and saunas. We moved there in 2005, when I was fifteen. During my time living in the compound, there were many changes: new restaurants opened, the grocery store was upgraded and a bowling alley established. When we moved in, there was a small, one-room library in the smallest, least popular leisure centre. This room did not see much foot traffic and I spent a lot of time there. The books were donated by the residents and a lot of them were romance or adult novels which could be considered inappropriate for young teens. I read them all.

Women drove freely within these walls and did not wear *abayas* (the black robe). The usual rules did not apply here.

The laws of compounds changed when an American couple were caught holding hands and walking together by some *mutawas* (moral police). The moral police took offence and asked the married couple to behave appropriately. As it turned out, the man was a high-ranking official in the new oil company set up in the country. To avoid further offending either party, it was decided that no moral police would be allowed into the expat compounds. In exchange, no Saudis could live in these compounds either.

Not only did we not wear *abayas* in my compound, women who wore them were not allowed to enter any of the three leisure centres, lest they ruin the carefully constructed delusions created especially for westerners in the compound. Nothing was to remind them that women were not actually free.

One time, Papa took his Saudi friend to a restaurant in our compound. While they were waiting to be seated, the waiter took Papa aside and told him that the friend, who was in traditional Saudi attire, was going to be a problem.

'Can you believe that?' Papa asked incredulously when he narrated the incident to us later that evening.

'What did you do?' Mama asked.

'There wasn't much I could do. I requested that they make an exception this time. It would have been too embarrassing otherwise.'

'Imagine telling a Saudi man that he isn't allowed in a restaurant in his own country.' Papa shuddered at the thought and decided never to put himself in such a position again.

This was the late 2000s and the *mutawas* still held a lot of the power when it came to moral policing in public. By this point, gender segregation in public spaces was common and even personal gatherings were segregated, including family weddings. Hospitals, banks and schools were also expected to follow this segregation. The compounds were the only places where these rules did not apply.

When the movement of Saudi women gained momentum in the early 1980s, the Higher Council of Ulama (established by royal decree to serve as a guardian of the piety of the nation) felt the need to monitor it. They also enforced male guardianship laws which forbade women from travelling, seeking employment, opening a bank account, marrying or divorcing, and undergoing certain medical procedures without their male guardian's permission.

The council also felt the need to segregate Saudi women from Western women so as not to corrupt the former. This was another reason why Saudis were not welcome in our compound. Moreover, Saudi children were not allowed to study in international schools. In these ways, we remained separated from the Saudis and the Saudis from us. There was also the language barrier to consider.

When I was twelve, Papa's Saudi colleague invited us over for dinner. The women ushered us in through a separate entrance and took us to a living room away from where the men sat. Without Papa to translate for us, Mama and I were lost. My sister was still a child and my brother was with Papa. We had

to rely on smiling, nodding and laughing as a way of communication. The hours stretched ahead of us. When Papa finally
called for us, we could not wait to leave. When we got in the
car and asked Papa why he took so long, he was surprised and
reminded us that it was barely 9 p.m.

Because of the lack of free mixing between expats and
Saudis, the former never had a fair chance to learn the
language. This made it difficult for expat women to navigate
life outside their homes even when the moral policing laws
were relaxed.

For my final two years of schooling, I moved from the Indian
girls' school to a British co-ed school. I was struggling to meet
the minimum requirements at the Indian school as there were
over fifty students in each class and the teachers could not
pay individual attention to each of us. I also didn't have much
aptitude for science subjects. I needed extra help and most
teachers offered private tuition after school and encouraged
students to attend these sessions. Papa was not comfortable
sending me to tuition in the evenings because the sessions
were mostly co-ed. To avoid this 'free mixing' he decided to
move me to a new school. Even though the school was co-ed,
he was confident that the constant supervising would keep
the students in check.

My new school was much smaller and the curriculum was
British. It was also a lot more flexible than my previous school
and I assumed this meant I would be able to pick the subjects
I wanted to study. In the Indian school, there was a stigma
attached to arts and commerce subjects – most Indian parents
pushed their children to study STEM (Science, Technology,
Engineering and Mathematics) subjects. In the new school, you
could pick a combination of subjects, but before I could make
up my mind, Papa picked Maths, Chemistry and Physics for

me. English Language was compulsory. He told me I could skip Biology if I wanted. I did. I chose English Literature instead.

Academically, these two years were challenging for me. Just when I had decided that education was going to be my way out of my community's limited thinking, I was forced to confront my ineptitude. For a while, I tried to convince my father to let me study liberal arts, but his heart was set on making me an engineer. I knew I wasn't going to fare well in an engineering college and that my best bet would be to get a BA and find a job in the creative industry, maybe even journalism. It felt terribly unfair that I could not work towards this ambition with the subjects of my choice, a decision that almost jeopardised my chance to attend the university I wanted most.

Another change was the multinationalism. In my previous school all students were Indians. After more than fifteen years in the country, I still had not befriended anyone outside of the South Asian community. As with international compounds, Saudis were not allowed to attend international schools but there were several Middle Eastern and Asian students. Right away I noticed a divide on grounds of nationality and language. I missed the strong sense of community I felt in my old school; we all shared a language and an understanding. We shared similar backgrounds and parental expectations.

I had to make new friends, navigate co-education in an environment highly policed by supervisors whose only job was to ensure there was no co-ed mingling, and to relearn my nonchalance towards beauty. The latter became more challenging in a co-ed school.

After two years of struggling with my A Levels and constantly vocalising my wish to stay away from engineering, Papa finally gave in. My results spoke volumes too and he had to concede that I was not designed for engineering after all. I expressed a wish to study journalism, but Papa said this was not a fitting career for a Muslim girl. I flitted between subjects before landing on geopolitics.

In 2008, Jeddah did not have full-time universities that taught in English. I remember this final year of school being one of chaos and confusion. Papa thought I was too young for the Western world and it was decided that I would pursue my education in India.

This suited me just fine. My yearly trips to India had warmed me to the place and I felt that the country's sense of freedom and openness (when compared to Saudi Arabia) would help me thrive. I looked forward to being on my own, away from home for the first time. While I stayed focused on what my future held for me, I failed to notice how things were changing for some of my friends.

My classmates from the British school were applying to multiple universities in the US and the UK, but my friends from the Indian school were embarking on different journeys altogether. Several parents were reluctant to let their daughters study away from home, even at the risk of not educating them. The lack of English universities in Jeddah meant that some of my friends had to settle for distance learning degrees in the humanities. Others were married as soon as they turned eighteen. While still teenagers, they moved from their parents' homes to their in-laws', having their first child a year later.

Some of my friends moved back to India to study engineering or dentistry. Their parents let them go on the condition that they live with relatives and follow a strict curfew. Some others were allowed to study if they married first and then went to the same university as their new husbands. I believe the girls' parents took on the responsibility of funding both their degrees.

At seventeen, I understood that pursuing dreams came with

many conditions, and parents did not want to do anything that could jeopardise their daughter's marriageability. Among such norms, my parents made the 'brave' decision to let me pursue my higher education in India without the presence of male guardians.

Part Two
Manipal

I applied for a BA in Geopolitics at Manipal University. I was accepted. A career in geopolitics felt like a step away from becoming a journalist, but as I approached my leaving date, I found myself excited about my decision. I could always become a foreign correspondent, I reasoned.

Manipal was a small university town only a couple of hours away from Honnavar. There was campus security in place and student accommodation was gender segregated with strict curfews. This filled my father with confidence. I was happy to study in a small town, having never crossed a street on my own nor left the house without a chaperon for seventeen years.

My start date at the university coincided with my family's summer break, which we traditionally spent in India. This meant that when I left home for the first time, my entire family came with me. Though I had waited a long time to leave, I was not ready to say goodbye to Saudi Arabia when the day finally arrived. I remember feeling scared and knowing deep down that I would miss home. My hair loss was not improving, and Mama worried that students might bully me for it. Her biggest concern was that someone might pull my bandana off or that my roommates might notice my thinning hair and be mean about it. This fear was starting to rub off on me and overshadowed the excitement I was feeling.

We arrived in India a couple of weeks before freshers' week. I spent this time feeling both nervous and excited. I had never lived in India without my parents. Almost all interactions that I had had with the country was through them. When we travelled within India, I stayed close to my father, the noises and the crowds overwhelming me. In Bangalore, I worried that maybe living on my own in India was not the best choice after all. Maybe I still needed my parents.

Before I could decide, I received an email from the university saying that they had cancelled the geopolitics course because not enough students had enrolled but that they could transfer me to the journalism or business school. I did not care for business and Papa was not keen on journalism. I could not imagine another three years of studying subjects I was not interested in, but what scared me the most was the thought of having to take a gap year because it was now too late to apply anywhere else. Even though I was feeling apprehensive about living in India on my own, I already knew I couldn't go back to the restrictive life in Saudi Arabia.

I sat with this news for a while, mulling over my options and trying not to panic. I asked myself if this was the push I needed to stand up for what I wanted. Maybe it was time to not let others decide for me.

The journalism course was set to start on the same day as the now cancelled geopolitics course. The business course had started a couple of weeks ago. Before I went to my parents with the news, I knew that not only was I going to have to fight to study in Manipal, I also had to make sure that I enrolled in the journalism school. My faith in Allah was strong, and I believed that this last-minute change was an answer to my prayers, a result of all the times I went to Makkah (or Mecca as it is known to some) and prayed for a chance to study what I wanted. When I finally revealed the change of plans to my parents, Mama did not say anything, but as expected Papa suggested that I opt for the business degree.

'I do not want to,' I said. 'It is already two weeks in and I will never catch up or make friends.' Papa suggested we consider other universities, preferably Bangalore, where we had family. I said I would only study in Manipal, the pounding of my heart filling my ears. 'Let's talk about it later,' Papa said. We were in the car and Papa was mindful of the presence of my aunt and my best friend from Jeddah who had already started college in the neighbouring state and was visiting me in Bangalore. This did not feel like an appropriate setting to stand my ground, but I also knew if I didn't speak now, I might lose the courage I had mustered. I slumped in my seat and declared that I was not going anywhere but Manipal. I had never seen him that angry. He lost his temper at me for being stubborn and started scolding me. My friend looked out of the window and my aunt fiddled with the clasp of her purse. Mama watched me intently. I still remember the shame I felt that day, being humiliated in front of my closest friend. But I also knew that I could not let this get in the way of my resolve, not when I was so close to my dreams coming true. Later that evening, Papa agreed and I emailed the university to let them know that I would be joining their journalism school. My first revolt was a success. I celebrated in silence.

I left for Manipal with Mama, Papa and my siblings. It was in the middle of the monsoon season and the air was humid. When we arrived, the place was crowded with parents and freshers; the seniors were not expected for another couple of weeks. For months I had been trying to imagine what Manipal would be like and finally I was here. It was love at first sight.

I was stunned by the architecture, a mixture of old and new. The biggest campuses were reserved for the medical and engineering students. The journalism school was tiny in comparison, a cluster of unique buildings, some recently built and others refurbished from an old factory. Because our college was small, the journalism students did not have their own halls; we shared with the engineering students. The student accommodation I was housed in had thirteen floors with at least seventy rooms on each floor. I was surprised by how modern the rooms were. Before Manipal, I'd had a biased view of India. This was because of my limited exposure to Indian cities and having spent most of our summer breaks in small towns.

Papa opted for me to have a shared room because he had had a good experience in shared accommodation when he was a student. The room was cramped, but I loved the view of the lush valleys and trees from the thirteenth floor.

On our first day in Manipal, Mama took over the task of helping me settle in. We went to the neighbouring town of Udupi where she picked out some essentials for me.

That evening when we returned to my accommodation to drop off my new possessions, we found some of my future classmates sitting on the stairs leading up to the hostel reception. When Mama walked up the stairs, I noticed all the girls watching her. Later when I became friends with one of the girls on the stairs, she told me about how she would always remember the first time she saw my mother. 'She looks like royalty,' my friend told me. 'Regal' was the word she used.

The morning of my orientation, I woke up alone in my dorm room, got dressed and had breakfast at the mess. I then waited in the reception for my family to pick me up. At the time I did not think it weird that my parents would attend orientation with me; there were other parents in the audience too. I should have worried more about my sister who was nine at the time and spent most of the welcome address trying to open a crisp packet and being noisy in the process. I was red with embarrassment and avoided the gaze of other students who looked around to find the source of the noise.

My family stayed on when my classes commenced and I got used to seeing them for lunch between my lessons. I was getting anxious about saying goodbye to them and wondered how it would be to say goodbye to Mama. I fixated over what I would tell her and if I should hug her. I could not remember the last time I had and worried that the farewell would be awkward. I was going to miss her terribly, but there was no space in our relationship to express this. I did not know how Mama was feeling. Like me, she kept up the pretence that nothing was changing.

On the third day of classes, as I stepped out for lunch, I called Papa to ask where they would like to eat today. Papa said that they were already halfway to Honnavar and that they had decided to leave because they could see that I was now settled. I had to hold back my tears in the college court-yard, conscious of my new classmates around me. 'Okay,' I said. 'Have a safe journey.' 'You be good,' Papa said. Instead of feeling relieved, I felt regret. I wanted to say a proper goodbye to the people who were my home for seventeen years.

Growing up, I did not have much in the name of conventional freedom and this move away from Saudi Arabia liberated me in ways I never thought would be possible. My time in Manipal was the most immersive experience of my life. For the first time I had my own library card and access to every shelf in that library. I spent endless hours sitting on the cold tiled floor between shelves, finishing one book and picking another. After the years spent in Jeddah reading books such as Sidney Sheldon's suspense novels, every copy of the Olsen twins' stories, and R. L. Stine's *Goosebumps* series, I was ready for what I imagined was 'serious' literature. However, looking back, the books I read in Jeddah set a strong foundation for my storytelling. Back home – because of the limited number of books – I did not have the luxury of picking a favourite genre. I read every book that I came across, from children's books, to sci-fi, to books for adults and books based on popular TV series. In Jeddah, I encountered *Star Wars* as a graphic novel before realising that the images in the book were from the films.

In my college library, I worked my way systematically through the aisles because that is how I read. It took me a while to realise that there were too many books here and I could read what I wanted without having to worry about reading them all. But old habits die hard and in my second semester, I found myself in the poetry aisle. I had never come across poetry books before and was not sure what to expect. Philip Larkin's poetry made me laugh. I did not understand T.S. Eliot. I stayed away from the epics and I did not know what to make of Ted Hughes. I knew I was not reading them right and just when I was ready to move on to the next aisle, I came across Sylvia Plath. Her words hit me like shrapnel. I understood every feeling she was expressing. I felt the silences in between her words too; they introduced a new dimension to my existence, a place where I could withdraw to when the world became unbearable. I could not get enough of her.

Plath also helped me understand motherhood beyond the expectations my society placed on it. At the time, I didn't know any other writer who had dissected the conflicted reality of being a mother with such honesty. I was horrified at first but quickly mellowed. I saw my own mother in her words. This was the beginning of my journey in trying to unravel the mystery of Mama. Until this point in my life, I had simply assumed that mothers enjoyed every aspect of motherhood.

I felt entitled to Mama's unconditional love and I refused to see her beyond her role as a mother. Plath made me see Mama as a woman, and that was the beginning of my journey to understand both these women.

Since moving away from home, I hardly spoke to Mama. I missed her desperately, but I didn't have the language to tell her. One time we went forty-five days without speaking. I oscillated between anger and self-pity, but I never thought to call her. I wanted to be loved but I wasn't willing to let her love me.

Through my readings, I confronted the idea that maybe motherhood didn't come naturally to Mama after all, at least not in a way my culture perpetuated it. I also felt that Mama was struggling between being the mother she wanted to be and being the mother she was expected to be. She worried about how her children behaved in public and she herself behaved differently around people. Her anxiety about what people might think of her mothering emanated from her. At home, with just the family, she was more relaxed and forgiving. This led to contradictions and an unpredictability that always made me agitated around her. I could not guess how Mama might react nor could I rely on an established pattern of predictable outcomes to help me relax at home. I spent my teenage years on edge, and I think so did Mama. I wondered how different our relationship would be if she was allowed to be herself, my mother.

My classes were from nine to five, five days a week, with occasional half-days on Saturdays. I sat near the front of the class and I paid attention. Our year was divided into two sections and soon I came to be known as the nerd in my class. This was a new experience for me and I thrived under this label. I did all my homework, I raised my hand to answer the teacher's questions, I prompted class discussions and I became an overall pain in the neck for everyone around me.

I enjoyed my lessons and applied myself. I was no longer at the bottom of my class. My teachers and classmates too recognised my writing and reporting skills. I studied gender theory, Shakespeare, history and visual communication. I learned how to shoot and edit films, and I spent hours at the computer lab perfecting my Photoshop skills. I dabbled with animation, art history, economics and radio presentation. Most importantly, I was around people who did not reduce my ambition down to a cute hobby, but saw it as the means to a viable career path.

I spent this time wide-eyed and in awe. I went from a shortage of people to an avalanche of them. They were everywhere, and they were approachable, regardless of gender. I made friends at my college, in student halls, at the food court, on the streets. I met like-minded people and I met Indian students who had lived all around the world. Manipal was a popular destination for children of non-residing Indians and it was interesting to learn about their experiences in America, Europe and Asia. The engineering students were settling in and the halls were teeming with girls. The girls' dorms were situated in between the colleges and the boys' dorms and the street outside my accommodation became a hangout spot for a lot of us. After a quick prepaid dinner at the mess, I would spend time with friends, making sure I was always back in my accommodation before the 9 p.m. curfew.

Possibly the most life-changing experience of all was to suddenly be surrounded by so many independent and confident young women who had travelled on their own, worked at NGOs, and had big dreams for their future without the pressures of getting married first. These women were pursuing their dreams in various fields and did not seem to be limited by their family. I had assumed that all Indian families watched over their daughters like hawks but most of my friends' parents were relaxed, understanding and engaged in their daughter's upbringing.

In Saudi Arabia, I had tried to make peace with the eventuality of education-marriage-children as a life plan. I knew the rules. I was to get an education, but just enough to make me a viable candidate on the marriage market. Anything more than a bachelor's could intimidate a potential husband and more importantly, it would indicate that I was interested in a career, which automatically meant I would not make a good wife or mother. It was easier to come to terms with this at school because I was not enjoying what I was studying. After two years of Maths, Physics and Chemistry, I was ready to give up and give in. That changed when I moved to India to study Journalism and Communication. Manipal became my happy place and I could not believe my luck.

When I needed a dose of reality, Honnavar was just a few hours away. I tried to visit every semester and while I enjoyed seeing my grandparents, my extended family continued living in the past, fixated on my hair loss and my marriage prospects. My hair loss was still a mystery to the family and after years of hiding it from their prying eyes, I did not know how to be honest about it. I shrugged, pushed away questions and sometimes even ducked when people tried to pull at my hair to see if it was real. In these moments, I missed Mama the most. I knew she would never let these people near me if she was around. I felt vulnerable being away from her, trying to exist without her.

At home in Jeddah, I had distanced myself from the idea of beauty, but in Manipal I realised that I liked dressing up. Not being limited to a black robe probably helped. I took an interest in what I wore and how I wore it. In Jeddah, Mama usually helped me choose my clothes or commented on a new outfit; her approval meant a lot to me and I always kept this in mind when buying clothes. But in Manipal, without this mental barrier, I could pick the clothes I wanted and not worry about what Mama would like. To her credit, Mama much preferred my Manipal wardrobe to my Jeddah clothes and once even asked me what had changed. I did not have the heart to tell her that it was this new distance between us which was giving me the confidence to be myself. It was my first lesson in the importance of trusting my instincts and not letting others' opinions change the way I behave.

While in Jeddah I had worn a scarf to hide my hair loss, I did not want to wear a scarf in India because I was conscious of being a minority in my home country. In Saudi Arabia, a hijab was a natural extension of a woman's attire, but not in India. There were women who wore the hijab in Manipal, but they were rare. I didn't want to stand out for wearing one, especially because my intentions were not religious. I felt that women who wore the hijab were perceived in a certain way by others and I let this fear guide me. I decided to wear bandanas instead.

The bandanas I wore were not the traditional square-shape but headbands with excess fabric. The bandana covered most of my head and gathered at the nape of my neck with elastic. I tied my hair in a ponytail which was visible from underneath the bandana. Later, I realised that a lot of my peers had assumed that this was my version of the hijab.

In Manipal, no one questioned the fact that I always wore a bandana. I had a collection to match my outfits and was never seen without one. At the freshers' party, which I did not attend, the seniors labelled every fresher with an attribute. Some flattering, some not so. A female friend of mine was called 'catwalk auntie'. I was not sure what it meant but I remember how much it upset her. A male friend was labelled 'gentleman'. This meant so much to him that he carried the little green card with the label in his wallet for years after and even showed it to me once. I was labelled 'Ze-band'. It was the only reference anyone ever made to my bandana in Manipal.

I was also free of the constant reminders of not being beautiful enough. Here, I felt beautiful, truly and utterly. I was free of Mama's penetrating gaze and the 'tragedy' of my hair loss. I started seeing myself for who I was and not how Mama saw me. At home, I would sometimes catch Mama watching me. She would look at me with an intensity that pricked at my skin. I felt visible and invisible at the same time. This staring usually ended with her in tears.

In Manipal, my looks did not cause anyone any tears. In Saudi Arabia I was an outsider, undesirable. In India, I caught people's attention and I was complimented for my appearance. I was growing into my skin, and the confidence I felt was palpable.

When I left home, Papa bought me my first laptop and now there was no time limit on being online. I tired of Facebook soon enough and instead spent my time trying to understand the world. I began with a question that took up most of my headspace: my difficult relationship with Mama. I came across works by Audre Lorde, Simone de Beauvoir and Rachel Cusk. I learned that motherhood can be a dark experience and that difficult relationships between mothers and daughters are more common than my family and friends were willing to accept. I read parts of *The Feminine Mystique* by Betty Friedan and couldn't stop wondering if Mama experienced the world as described by Friedan.

I went back home at the end of each semester. This travelling back and forth every few months kept things firmly in perspective. It was a reminder of how precarious my fate was. What was so easily given could just as easily be taken away.

Manipal felt like an unreal interlude in the real life which was waiting in the wings to take over as soon as I graduated. This was probably why I never took my time in Manipal for granted and pushed myself constantly towards new experiences. I was still painfully shy then, but I didn't let it get in the way of interacting with people. This did not help with my social anxiety and some nights I spent hours lying awake, obsessing over something silly I had said or done that day.

Papa faced resistance from his peers when he decided to let me study away from home. Some of his friends were getting their daughters married after high school and others were making them study via distance learning. In between semesters, I met a friend who had recently married. She was pregnant then, but reluctant to tell me. I asked her why she got married so young. The last time we had met she was applying to study fashion. She said the reason she got married was because her parents were getting tired of putting off *rishtas* (matrimonial requests that usually lead to arranged marriages). This stayed with me. Grown-ups who were so averse to asserting themselves that they would rather marry off their only daughter than say no. My recent reading habits were also making me aware of the social and power dynamics of marriage and parenthood. These were no longer options without serious consequences, the way the elders in my community projected them to be.

My new friends were helping me broaden my horizons. There were no cinemas in Saudi Arabia in the 1990s and 2000s and I had mainly watched Indian TV shows or Bollywood movies featuring lovestruck heroes, damsels in distress, and dance sequences shot in Switzerland, none of which related to my teenage years in any way. In fact, not seeing myself in books, films, or on TV ended up making me feel more alone. With its strict censorship laws, Saudi Arabia had also played a part in keeping a lot of the real world from me. I did not know about the various feminist movements, the AIDS crisis in the 80s, or the existence of the LGBT+ community, let alone the strides they had made over the decades. These topics were not discussed and there wasn't much knowledge about it among my school friends. No religion except Islam was allowed to be publicly practised in Saudi Arabia. When I left the country, I had to learn not only to secularise my language, but also my thought process. Even just acknowledging others' religious views became a conscious effort on my part.

My peers in Manipal were also a lot more politically aware and I believe that growing up in countries that respected free speech made a difference to their engagement. In Saudi Arabia, people didn't freely engage in political conversations and to date, writers and activists are punished for speaking out against the monarchy. Mama is constantly nervous about my choice to be vocal about my experiences, and fears that I might offend my home country.

After I left home, I had a chance to experience movies at the cinema and to watch off-beat, indie movies. Indie productions were a completely new art form for me. I spent hours binge-watching old films which I borrowed from the library, as well as American sitcoms that everyone around me had already watched. I remember *Gossip Girl* becoming popular and though the premise did not interest me at first, I ended up devouring the first season. I started the first episode before bed and was hooked immediately. Although I kept promising myself that the next episode would be the last one, before I realised it, it was morning and time for me to get ready for college. I had stayed up all night, engrossed in the lives of the Upper East Side. These lives were so different from mine; I could not help but watch their stories unfold. Watching New York on-screen, I also became enthralled by the Metropolitan Museum of Art and it became a sight I desperately wanted to see in person.

Looking back at my time in Manipal, I realise that I do not have many stories. I think this is because not a lot was actively happening to me. I was an open-mouthed spectator watching the world come alive around me. I read books I had only previously heard of, I perused magazines from cover to cover, everything from *The Economist* to the *New Yorker*. I read *Vogue* and *Harper's*. I read *People* magazine (the Indian version) and I read newspapers.

If I were to describe how I felt during this time in one word, it would be 'overwhelmed'. There was so much I did not know. I had not heard about the Holocaust nor fully understood the impact of slavery in America before moving to Manipal. History lessons at school primarily focused on Indian or Islamic history so both these events came as a shock to me. I became conscious of my lack of general knowledge and sought out books that would help me understand modern history. The more I read about the world, the more I thought about my own place within it. Trying to learn about our past helped me make sense of who I was. I discovered how small I was in comparison to all that had come before me. Until then, I had approached life from my limited perspective, but now I was keen to stop placing my experiences at the centre of every discourse I engaged in. There was a world outside of mine, a world waiting to be discovered.

When my friends went partying in the evenings, I stayed in my room reading my books and waiting for Papa's call. Like me, most of the Manipal students were away from home for the first time. This newfound freedom meant different things to different people. For some it was about circumventing the curfew to stay out late, get drunk, smoke weed or hook up. For others it was about challenging themselves, becoming politically active, fighting for the causes they believed in and staying true to their principles. A lot of my peers were able to strike a balance between the two.

For me, it was about asserting control over myself. It was about choosing the food I ate, the clothes I wore, the people I surrounded myself with and the kind of energy I projected. It was about getting to know myself without the superficial pressures to appear a certain way. It was about learning from my mistakes and confronting my fears.

I truly believed I was living my best life when I met Anna, a Norwegian exchange student who was in Manipal for a few weeks. She was allotted a room on my floor but spent most evenings in my room where the Wi-Fi connection was better. On her first night in the dorm, at 9 p.m. on the dot, I hurried her to the reception, so we could sign in and record our presence. She found the whole thing very funny but came along when I insisted that these were the rules.

At the reception, I signed against my name under the watchful eyes of at least five wardens whose job it was to make sure we signed under the correct name. In an hour, they would be knocking on the doors of those who had failed to sign. Anna asked the warden what would happen if she was not in the building by 9 p.m. I translated the conversation for both Anna and the warden. 'We will call your parents,' the warden said. I repeated the threat in English. This made Anna laugh. 'Please do,' she said, 'I have been travelling for a while now and my parents do not even know which town I am in, they would love to hear from you.'

I was too scared to translate this back to the warden but I remember being struck by this independence, which was new to me. A life where I was not answerable to my parents for my every move? I couldn't imagine it. While Anna laughed in the face of these rules, I stayed in my room and diligently waited for Papa's call every evening to report to him about my day and confirm that I was indeed in my room and ready for bed.

There were many things Saudi Arabia didn't prepare me for and one of them was that I will always meet people who will have many questions about living in Saudi Arabia. There is so much written about it that people assume they know what it is like to live there. And when they meet someone like me, they are quick to foist their misconceptions on me. They are quick to assume my experiences and my feelings towards my home country and often struggle to come to terms with my love for Jeddah. I was also stunned by how deeply the Saudi culture had infiltrated people's understanding of the Islamic teachings.

Distance from home gave me the space to ask some difficult questions without the guilt of committing blasphemy.

In Jeddah, when I questioned certain aspects of Islam, people were quick to shut me down and insist that I say, '*Astaghfirullah*' ('I seek forgiveness from Allah') three times. While I repeated the word, I wondered how a religion based on seeking knowledge and interpreting our faith had turned into a totalitarian undertaking.

I realised that I did not subscribe to the tyrannical, homophobic and misogynist Islam I was exposed to in my early years. I was only just embarking on my feminist journey and I was keen to marry Islam with it. To me, feminism has always been about everyone's choice to be their true selves, and I knew that in its original form, this is what Islam preached as well. The Qur'an is wide open for interpretation and encourages Muslims to take from it what they will. It gives Muslims a mission: create a just and decent society, in which everyone is treated with respect. Most Muslims have one thing in common, our deep and unwavering love for our Prophet. Our religion requires us to strive to understand our Prophet's life and apply this understanding to our own.

Growing up, every iteration of the Prophet's life came tinged with the speaker's intention to subjugate women. Women's inequality was the foundation of the patriarchal structure, but it was legitimised with misogynistic interpretations of Islam. The culture dictated how the Qur'an was interpreted and I didn't find an unbiased retelling of our Prophet's life until I read Karen Armstrong's book, *Muhammad*. It amuses me that my understanding of Islam didn't come from my years in Saudi Arabia but from a liberal white woman of Christian faith. Armstrong didn't have a point to prove, or a mind to change, just a story to tell. Reading her clear and balanced book on my Prophet's life made me realise that I needed to seek scholars who would help me interpret my religion for myself, the way Islam was intended to be followed.

Muslims believe that the Qur'an came to our Prophet in chapters, through an angel. We call them revelations. The first word of the first revelation is *iqra*. It means read. The Qur'an starts with a command to seek knowledge. To me, this means Muslims are an *ummah*, a community, tied by their pursuit of knowledge. But every time I questioned our culture, the word *fitna* was thrown at me. *Fitna* means rebellion and in this context, it means rebelling against my religion, against Allah. At first this scared me, but I realised that if your faith is threatened by a young girl's questioning, maybe it's time to revisit your values. And if your faith excludes one gender's happiness and freedom, is it a faith worth fighting for?

My religion is above the culture I had grown up in. This was the first realisation in my pursuit of understanding Islam. My religion is better than the people who oppress their women in the name of Islam. My religion is better than the men who proclaim themselves to be scholars in public, yet abuse women and young boys in private. My religion is better than the men who tell me to cover myself while they uncover women without their consent.

I had seen too many Muslim women believe that submission to man is equal to submission to God. And if that's not blasphemous, I don't know what is.

From a young age I was taught to recognise danger. My early experiences with groping and the stories I heard about sexual assault had made me a vigilant person. I was aware of the spaces I occupied and was ready to leave them the moment I felt unsafe, without feeling apologetic for it. And it was probably because of this that I thought I knew what danger looked like. I was in for a surprise.

The 'danger' arrived in the form of a famous media personality invited to speak at our college festival. Traditionally, the final year students hosted the festival and students from other years helped execute their vision. I signed up to help with hospitality. This meant I would get to meet some of the amazing speakers who were travelling to Manipal from across the country for this festival. I was given a list of names and my job was to ensure the speakers were at the college in time for their event. I worked with an itinerary and moved between airport, hotel and college with a self-important frenzy. My Jeddah self would not have recognised this person who was in such control of her movements.

Things were going well and on the last day of the festival I waited outside the college gates to greet the last speaker of the festival. I introduced myself to him and instead of responding, he looked me up and down and nodded. I walked him to the green room and waited with him until he was called on stage.

He entered the hall to an uproar of applause. This man was popular. He spoke well and answered several audience questions. He had a presence about him that was magnetic. He stayed to take pictures with the students and when the crowd thinned, he walked up to where I was waiting for him. My last task of the day was to take him downstairs to where the food stalls were in the college courtyard. It was 6 p.m. and the evening crowd was starting to arrive. I showed him all the food options and said my goodbye, including how grateful I was for this opportunity to spend time with him.

He looked around while I was talking and made a face. 'Nothing looks good here, why don't you take me to your favourite restaurant?' he asked. This made me uncomfortable, but I was not sure how to get out of the situation. There were lots of people around me and I did not want to leave the safety of this crowd. I tried to make an excuse about meeting friends for dinner and he asked me to invite them too. I frantically texted two of my male friends, thinking that their gender might protect me. Both were in their individual dorm rooms and did not want to come out. I pleaded with them to join me as I got in the autorickshaw with the man. I just needed one of them to be there. Both turned up in the end and were waiting for us at the restaurant when we arrived.

It was the most awkward dinner. The man was annoyed with my friends and kept ignoring them, focusing his attention on me. My friends did not know what to talk about. Both were engineering students and had no idea who this man was. We ordered in silence and when the evening ended, the man asked me to drop him off at his hotel. By now, because of his rudeness and his unwavering focus on me, even my friends were starting to feel that I was not safe around him. They suggested that one of them could walk me to my dorm and the other friend could drop the man off at his hotel. He rejected this suggestion and pointed at the waiting autorickshaw, gesturing at me to get in.

Without my knowledge, my friends got in the next autorickshaw and followed us to the hotel. I was scared of what he might say when we arrived at our destination. I kept telling myself that I was still in control of this situation and that I did not have to do anything I did not want to. But then I remembered that I did not want to go to dinner with him nor be in this autorickshaw.

He got out and was about to say something when he noticed my friends getting out of the rickshaw behind ours. The man said goodnight and went into the hotel. I got out of the rickshaw, paid the driver and walked to my halls with my friends.

That night the man texted me a few times. He asked me to meet him the next morning at the hotel for breakfast because he wanted to give me some books. He knew I was interested in publishing as a profession. He mentioned that he had friends at HarperCollins and that he would like to introduce me to them. He said he could see potential in me. I had never met anyone who worked in publishing before and this felt like a great opportunity.

But I was terrified of what he might say at breakfast. I often wonder why I did not just ignore his texts, but in that moment, this did not feel like an option. I do not think I knew that I could say no. I messaged my friends my where-abouts and asked them to check in every half hour via text. I decided that I would walk out if I felt uncomfortable.

When I got to the hotel, I found him sitting in the lobby, the books in front of him. I was relieved. I was worried that he would pretend to forget the books and ask me to come to his room with him. That was going to be my cue to leg it. We went to the hotel restaurant and he talked about his wife and children and how his wife was not his boss and that he could do anything he pleased.

I nodded in silence, listening, not uttering a word. There was no talk about publishing or anything related to my career. I am not sure if he could sense my discomfort, but the breakfast ended abruptly. He said goodbye and walked to the hotel reception. I walked out of the restaurant and felt free. I texted my friends to let them know that I was safe and started walking towards my college. Looking at the books he gave me, I decided to donate them to the library.

On this walk, I went over the last couple of days in my head and asked myself if I was imagining things. That maybe he was a good man and that maybe he did see potential in me and wanted to introduce me to his publishing friends. Just then I received a text. It was from him. It read, 'I didn't know Aquarians could be so beautiful.'

I decided to ignore the text. I spent the rest of the day in confusion, asking myself if I was somehow responsible for his actions. Did I lead him on? Was there anything I could have done differently? I was scared. I knew he was a powerful man and I wondered what he would do if I made him angry. A few hours later I thought it might be best to reply to his message after all. I ignored his comment and simply wished him a safe journey and thanked him for coming to our college. He did not reply.

I woke up the next morning to two missed calls from him, at 2 a.m. and 2.33 a.m. I knew this had to stop. There was a text message from him too, saying that he dialled by mistake. He messaged me for almost a month after that, threatening my career and implying that he had the power to ensure I never got a job in publishing in India. I believed this. But I was too scared to tell anyone about it. I did not reply to any of his messages and for a long time my phone triggered a sense of anxiety and fear. He eventually gave up and our paths never crossed again.

At eighteen, I didn't have the language to call him out on his behaviour. And this is exactly what he was relying on when he made his advances. In late 2018 when the #MeToo movement made waves in India, I was surprised by how many of the stories stemmed from this kind of behaviour. How aware these men are of their power and how they wield it to their advantage. And how – through it all – they still manage to make the vulnerable feel responsible for what's forced upon them.

Though I was in my home state, a lot about Karnataka was new to me. Before Manipal, I was only familiar with Honnavar, Sirsi and parts of Bangalore. Now I was getting to explore local towns and architecture. I was in awe of the old temples and I loved visiting my local friends. I accepted every invitation I received to meet my friends' parents; I spent time with their grandparents and I was fascinated by the architecture of their homes, especially the open courtyards and airy rooms, a change from the box flats and villas of Jeddah.

In their homes, I watched my female friends interact with their mothers, I observed the language in which they communicated. I watched mothers who openly doted on their daughters, mothers who shared an easy camaraderie and daughters who did not sulk at the slightest hint of teasing. I watched them being comfortable in each other's company, talking about their day and sharing their thoughts. This was a revelation to me, this possibility. Why could I not have this with my own mother?

Throughout my childhood, Papa was my friend. He was the one who listened, who seemed to care, who made time to talk about my dreams and the books I loved to read. His work took him away from his family for long stretches of time, but he did not let this get in the way of our time together. In fact, it gave us something to talk about, the places he visited and the people he met.

Papa had it all, a good job, a wife and three children, a house back in India and male privilege in Saudi Arabia. He took a risk when he moved away from home in his twenties and the risk paid off. Here he was, two decades later, providing for his growing family and supporting our comfortable life-style. I understood that Jeddah meant different things to him than it meant to me. I could see his point of view, but he could not see mine.

While I was in Jeddah, Papa convinced me that all good things were here. Ironic, considering how much he spoke of his travels and what he learned from meeting new people. When I left Jeddah, I saw the world from a different perspective. And I realised that what Papa wanted of me is not what I wanted for myself, not any more.

My self-study of Islam, feminism and history was creating a new foundation for me. All my old beliefs were cracking under the weight of these revelations. My religion was firm on knowledge being power. And to me, it was power to dream bigger and beyond other people's hopes for me.

When I left home at seventeen, I did not have the words to explain to my father that if I were to live and marry in Jeddah, my family too would heavily rely on me for free physical and emotional labour. I wanted to travel like my father; I did not want to spend the rest of my life listening to the stories of men in my family. I wanted to write my own.

After I came to terms with my self-identity as a Muslim woman, I had to come to terms with what this meant in relation to my identity as an Indian. Personally, I did not see any problem with being Indian, Muslim and female all at once but I became aware of others' attitudes towards me. The year I joined journalism school, the honorary director addressed the incoming class at orientation. He was in his eighties and talked to us wide-eyed aspiring journalists about his life and what he had learned about journalism over the years. He was a beloved journalist in India and the author of several books.

Over the course of our first semester, he gave us some tips, all of which I diligently noted down. One that has stayed with me is his advice to keep a notebook and to copy down interesting quotes and phrases that we come across in our reading and our lives. He became a role model with his quiet voice and gentle laughter. He came to college most days and unknown to me at the time, was working on two books, both of which were published in 2009.

I looked forward to running into him on campus. Most mornings, he could be seen slowly making his way from his office to the library. Students and teachers alike seemed to enjoy his presence and often one of us would stop to help him down a couple of steps or accompany him to and from the library. Once, during my first semester, I joined my classmates in the middle of a discussion about him and I announced that he was my role model. One of my classmates turned to me with a raised eyebrow. 'Why? Don't you know he is a Muslim hater?' Nothing I found online supported this claim, but hearing it changed something within me. I started avoiding him in the library. When I did help him down the steps, I did not spend the time engaging in any sort of conversation. While it might not have been true, the broader reality couldn't be ignored. Anti-Muslim sentiments were common in some parts of India and with the recent rise of far-right politics in the country, the sentiment had spread even wider.

In Jeddah, I mixed freely with Pakistani and Bangladeshi

immigrants without thinking about the origin of our differences. It was a normal part of my life. In India, the distance from these neighbours felt more pronounced. There were myths and misconceptions about them and there was an inclination to group all Muslims under one umbrella, regardless of nationality. Politicians questioned Indian Muslims' 'dual loyalty' and demanded proof of faithfulness to their birth country. Being Muslim felt at loggerheads with being an Indian citizen, but things hadn't always been this way for Indian Muslims. To understand how we became a divisive nation, I think it's important to understand the pre-independence politics of India.

The British started colonising India in the eighteenth century by displacing princely states and using artillery to subjugate land. From the early twentieth century onwards, they introduced what came to be known as the 'divide and rule' policy. This policy provoked communal distrusts and eventually led to the partition of British India on the basis of religious majorities. Due to the population of Muslim majorities in the north-east and north-west of India, British rulers carved them out to become East Pakistan (which later became Bangladesh) and West Pakistan. Both provinces were separate from each other and shared borders with India.

Being stuck on the 'wrong' side of the border caused mass hysteria and many families started migrating to India or Pakistan (depending on their faith) from the beginning of 1947. According to census reports from 1931 and 1951, 1.26 million Muslims and 0.84 million Hindus/Sikhs went missing during Partition. The violence against women during Partition was unprecedented. Even after Partition, the migration between the two countries continued well into the 60s and 70s. While Muslims feared being the minority in India, the Hindus fled Pakistan due to religious persecution.

It is impossible to discuss such a controversial and consequential subject in a few paragraphs, but the fact remains that Partition and the religious divide provoked by the British is the cause for much of the tension in the subcontinent even today. This truth soaks my country. I moved to India in 2008, six years after the fateful Gujarat riots. According to a BBC report from 2005, the 2002 riots ended with 1044 dead, 223 missing, and around 2500 injured, the majority being Muslims. The riots were inter-communal in nature and some of the worst in India's recent history of violence between Hindus and Muslims.

Karnataka, my home state, has seen a stark rise in communal violence in the last decade. Every violent incident is viewed politically, and the mainstream reaction differs depending on the victim's religion or caste. As a minority, this made me feel unsafe and unwelcome in my own country. On the cusp of adulthood and as a citizen of India, I was not sure how to come to terms with this insecurity. It seems my reaction was to distance myself from any public connections to my faith.

While I was trying to find my footing in India, the capitalist landscape of Saudi Arabia was changing. Many of my friends who had stayed behind to face their bleak prospects were now enrolling in one of the few English language universities that had recently opened in Jeddah. Women were slowly reappearing in public spaces and no longer restricted to hospitals and schools.

When I was home in the middle of my second year at university, Papa got me an internship at the local newspaper. It was my first time in an office environment and I worked closely with two female editors. They took me under their wing and gave me many opportunities to explore my interests and publish my articles. It boosted my confidence and made me consider print journalism as a viable career option. When I shared this with Papa, he was very happy. 'You can come back and work there after you graduate,' he told me. My heart sank.

I had left this life of gender segregation behind and was not keen on revisiting it. Having experienced non-segregated spaces, I did not understand why this should be an Islamic requirement. There was nothing about gender segregation in the Qur'an or the *hadiths* (the Prophet's sayings) but the subject still remains controversial within the Muslim community. There are scholars who believe that Muslims should not be segregated based on gender, especially as this was not the norm during our Prophet's lifetime. They cite the example of Makkah to support their claim. For years, Muslims of all genders have walked around the *Kabah* (the black cube-shaped structure at the centre Makkah) shoulder-to-shoulder. On the other side of the discussion are Saudi clerics who have issued a *fatwa* (religious ruling) calling for death warrants against people who do not respect the gender segregation.

In the past, Saudi Arabia leaned towards the more conservative thinking on gender segregation, and as a culture has enforced this upon all aspects of their citizens' lives. For a long time, doctors were not allowed to treat patients of the opposite gender. Now this is permissible if there are chaperones present, usually nurses. All restaurants in the country have a 'family section', but even within these shared spaces, barriers are present to help conceal the women further.

While I enjoyed my time interning at the newspaper, I found it difficult to readjust to the segregation which still very much exists, even if changes have taken place. The women were clustered together and were expected to keep their *abaya* on at all times, even in the building, even at our desks. If I wanted to use the toilet, I had to get a key from a senior female editor. The key locked the door that led to the cubicles so that no man could mistakenly enter and witness me coming out of a cubicle or washing my hands. Essentially, if I was using the toilet, no one else could. It felt like I was back in school, asking permission for something so simple.

I returned to Manipal after every break feeling grateful. I knew even then how lucky I was to experience such freedoms in college. The only thing I did not enjoy about Manipal was the weather. From September to February, the weather was mostly bearable. But from June to August, we would have one of the most extreme monsoons in the world. March to May were terribly hot and humid. A large portion of the student population in Manipal came from other parts of the country and most of us were not used to this weather. During the monsoon, it would rain continuously for days. Most mornings I would walk against the current, the sloped road leading up to my college flowing like a stream. Sometimes I would lose a flip-flop to this current and find myself running after it, an upturned umbrella pulling me in a different direction. Once, I remember being so exhausted that I simply stood and watched my flip-flop float away from me. I walked to class with one bare foot. In the summer, I took to carrying an extra T-shirt in my bag for when the one I was wearing was drenched in sweat.

I had never seen so much rain in my life and the humidity of coastal South India was a world away from the dry air of Saudi Arabia. When Papa signed me up for university accommodation, he opted for a non-AC room. I did not object. My childhood was different from my father's and he was constantly

98

worried that he was spoiling his children. He grew up without an AC and he thought I should learn to live without it too. In Manipal, I spent many sleepless nights with the windows open, willing the still, heavy air to gather speed. In the beginning, I repeatedly sought Papa's permission to shift to an AC room, and every time I asked, he brought up his own childhood, how he walked many kilometres to school, how he got one gift a year and how he made the most of his time outdoors. I understood the need to be aware of my roots, but I didn't understand what his childhood had to do with me lying awake in stifling heat.

In the middle of an oppressively still night, I went to the reception to wake one of the less strict wardens and asked to be put on the waiting list for an AC room. I then went upstairs and texted my father the difference he would have to pay for the room and tried to get some sleep before dawn. He replied, 'OK'.

I had always enjoyed a smooth relationship with my father, a contrast to my relationship with my mother. There were many reasons for this. Papa loved being a parent and I think it helped that he got to perform his role on his own terms. He was not responsible for the day-to-day chores that came with raising children. He didn't help us with our homework, he didn't wash up after us nor did he enforce a routine. That was left to Mama. He wasn't always around, and this gave us a chance to miss him. His homecoming was always a celebration. Papa had stories, he met people and he saw things that could be shared. Mama was always around and we rarely had anything to talk about. This made me think Mama was not interesting. It never occurred to me then how much she was giving up for the picture-perfect family Papa had imagined for himself.

Papa grew up with four brothers. I often wonder if his outlook on life would have been different if he had had a sister. Would he be a different kind of husband and father if he grew up around women and saw what it was like to be a woman in his family? Papa is the eldest and I am his first-born. When I was young, I remember Papa losing his temper quite easily. Maybe the pressure to provide for this family was too much for him in his early thirties. Maybe he just did not know how to be a father and was subconsciously copying the behaviour of others around him. By the time my sister was born, he mellowed and became the father I came to know and love. In my culture, there is pressure for men to be in control of everything and as I was growing up, I watched my father learning to let go and to start treating his wife and daughters as more than just his possessions. For me, this made Papa stand out from the other fathers. Though Papa was traditional and did seem to care about what others thought of us, he grappled with his biases a lot more consciously than his peers did. He had his fears, but he tried not to let them get in my way.

I was relying on his ability to put his biases aside when I applied for a scholarship to study in Germany for my final semester. I was nearing the end of my bachelor's and I was no longer the timid girl my parents had dropped off two years ago. I understood what a big decision it was for my parents to let me study in Manipal and while I appreciated this, I wanted more.

I can't remember how I mustered the courage to even imagine living on my own in Europe but I decided to give it a go. The application process was stringent and required me to create a dossier of my achievements. A few candidates were shortlisted and each of us was interviewed by what felt like the entire faculty of our college. It was a nerve-wracking experience, sitting at a long table across from the faculty members. I don't remember much from the interview except leaving the room feeling unsure of how the interview went.

We were told that the results would be announced within the next couple of weeks.

I checked the noticeboard every day for the list of four names to be revealed.

The nervousness in those two weeks made it difficult for me to eat or sleep. Even my parents could sense it. When I couldn't keep it to myself any longer, I told them about the opportunity and that I had applied. Papa was surprised, even enthusiastic, about the prospect of me living in Germany. Mama didn't say much.

When the two weeks were up, the results were still not announced. I knew an ex-student who was friends with some of the faculty members, so I asked him if he had heard anything. He said that they had been impressed with my interview but were put off by my low A Level grades. I thanked him for the information. I still hadn't forgiven Papa for making me study science subjects at A Level and felt renewed anger at this potential loss of opportunity.

A few days later, when I was in the library, a classmate came to congratulate me. The names had been announced that morning and I was on the list. I couldn't believe it and stayed in my seat, willing the news to sink in. That afternoon I called Papa to share the good news. I guess I was expecting congratulations, but instead Papa said, 'That's great but there is no need for you to go to Germany.' Those were his exact words. No need. I did not protest. The idea that I might *want* to do something was not up for discussion. After Papa hung up, I carried on with my day as though nothing had happened. My classmates and teachers continued to congratulate me throughout the day and I accepted their best wishes with as much graciousness as I could manage. Later that evening, when I was alone in my room, I cried. I cried for myself, but I also cried for all the broken dreams and the meaningless life ahead of me. I cried at my naivety.

I cried from the embarrassment of having to tell people in my college that I would not be able to accept the offer after all.

As I was getting ready for bed that evening, my phone rang. When I answered, it was Mama. I was not in the mood to talk and remained curt. Papa set the rules and I retaliated against Mama; this was how it had always been between us. Instead of a hello, I asked her what she wanted.

'Don't tell your teachers anything. Keep your place. I will talk to Papa,' she said.

This brief conversation with my mother was the first of its kind. It was an acknowledgement of how things worked in our family. To me it meant that she had always been aware of the gender disparity in our culture and our family but had chosen not to speak about it until this moment. I wasn't sure what to make of it, but it left an impression. Whatever the outcome, at least Mama was choosing not to be silent this time.

I woke up the next morning and carried on with my day as though nothing out of the ordinary had happened. I kept checking my phone but was not sure what I was waiting for. When I finished with the last class for the day, there was a missed call from Papa. I called back immediately.

'You can go to Germany,' he said.

This permission meant a huge deal even though there was a part of me that begrudged the need for such permission. But I decided to count my blessings and not make a scene. I wanted to appear grateful because I truly was.

I had always idealised the West, and a chance to study in a Western university meant I could gain experience and hopefully find the tools to create a space which was not at odds with my identity. In Saudi Arabia I was too Indian, too brown. In India I was too foreign, too Muslim. In a Western space, I thought I could be myself. That I could stand out and be celebrated for my differences. It would be a truly inclusive space, I thought.

Part Three
Bremen and Jeddah

Papa accompanied me on my first trip to Bremen from Jeddah. The other three students from my college had travelled from India a couple of weeks before I got there. I knew that no one else's parents had come to drop them off at the start of this programme, but I was too grateful to be embarrassed. I promised to test my comfort zone after I settled in Bremen.

It was no secret that Papa did not want me to go to Germany. But once it was decided that I was going, he did everything in his power to make sure that I had the best time in Europe. Papa worried that if something happened to me, he would not be able to help me the way he could in India or Jeddah. His network did not stretch as far as Germany. While this constant surveillance had annoyed me earlier, I realised that I too had come to rely on it. It had become a privilege that helped me feel safe wherever I went, until now.

Papa stayed with me in Bremen for a few days before going back to Jeddah. Bremen is a small city in the north-west of Germany, less than an hour away from Hamburg. My German friends told me it was one of the most populated cities in northern Germany but coming from India, it felt sparse to me. The town centre was a mixture of old and new architecture. Bremen used to be a major port along the River Weser but the historic buildings along the river were now occupied by art galleries or offices.

Papa and I explored parts of Bremen together and I could sense his nervousness about leaving me in this town. On our first day in Bremen, we went to my student accommodation directly from the airport. For the duration of the six months I stayed there, entering the building felt like I was stepping back in time. The décor was mostly shades of brown and the furniture looked like it was from the 50s. It probably was.

The student halls were a cluster of connected buildings and narrow hallways and I remember Papa's shock at the state of it. He asked me if I was sure that I could stay here. I nodded. It's not like I had options and surely I was not going to go back after coming so far. Years later, Papa confessed that it took a lot of effort on his part to not insist that I return to Jeddah with him after seeing the student accommodation.

The day Papa left, I cried. I had never felt so alone. It took me a while to understand that this was the price I had to pay for the independence I sought. When Papa was around, I stayed at the hotel with him and so the evening after his departure was the first time I slept in my own room. I fell on my bed, fully clothed, too tired even to get under my duvet cover. I heard the silence around me, a high-pitched note that surrounded me when my ears had nothing else to focus on. I propped myself on my elbows and leaned forward in bed until my hand reached the radiator. I switched it on and waited for the heat to disperse. The soft hiss of the heating was new to me, a change from the comforting hums of an AC. Another reminder of how far away I was from home.

I rolled over in bed and stared at the naked light bulb above my head. In Manipal, I always shared a room and at home, even though I had my own room, I rarely had any privacy. I pulled out my laptop from under my bed and googled the distance between Bremen and Jeddah. 3524.3 miles.

I fell asleep fully clothed and in the middle of the night, woke up with a start. I thought I heard Mama calling my name. When I was home, this usually meant a chore. It used to make me groan. That night it made me cry. The light was still on in the room. I sat in bed for a while, missing home, missing Mama. One day at a time, I promised myself. I changed into my pyjamas, switched off the light and tried to get some sleep before orientation day.

While I worried about how I would live in a new place, so far away from home and without the reassurance of grandparents living nearby, I was also fascinated by all that I saw around me. During my time there, I fell in love with the town centre and its statues from the fifteenth century, the old cathedral and the cobbled streets, especially Böttcherstraße, an iconic street famous for its unique architecture and landmarks.

The cobbled streets, the buskers, even the cold weather, all strangely reminded me of Bollywood dance sequences where the hero and heroine were whisked off to 'exotic' locations. I guess in that way, there was some familiarity. Bremen was much bigger than Manipal and there was a lot to take in as well. But it was quieter on my senses. The students I studied with were mostly in their late twenties and thirties, making them much older than my teenage classmates in Manipal. The weather, too, was kinder, rain came in gentle intervals and springtime added to the beauty of Bremen.

The university was a bus and a tram ride away from my accommodation. My schedule was light compared to my time in Manipal. I had a choice of lessons to select from, a small list of classes from the politics and journalism courses that were conducted in English. I opted for economics and politics subjects along with weekend courses in openness, creativity and perception. When I sent in my list of subjects to the administrator, she wanted to double-check that I definitely did not want to take up any journalism courses. I had failed to make a distinction between the two courses on the list. I stuck to my choices. Studying politics in a new country was an interesting experience. And with my lack of general knowledge I had a lot of catching up to do.

I enjoyed every subject I studied at Bremen. The reading material for each class was emailed to students a week in advance and I came prepared for the lessons, meticulously highlighting the set reading and coming in with a list of questions. In some classes, my English was more fluent than the other students' and even the teachers'. Often when we stopped to check the meaning of certain words, I would raise my hand to explain the definition or help with the pronunciation. The only subject I struggled with was German. My German teacher in Manipal was an enthusiastic but lenient man. In Germany, our teacher refused to speak in any language but German, giving me no choice but to try to understand her.

In between classes and in the evenings, I sought out other students from Manipal. The exchange programme included four of us in total. I had not been friends with any of them before I moved to Germany. Our circles were different, but being so far away from our familiar environment stripped us of our sense of social hierarchy and we became dependent on each other, if not friends.

We had chosen different subjects to study and our paths rarely crossed during the day except for lunch breaks. We met up in the evenings in one of our rooms and exchanged stories and shared discoveries. We talked about how to use the self-service stations, the best time to use the washing machines, which supermarket was most cost-effective and how to stay warm in the bitter cold. We exchanged notes on people who were kind and those who were a 'bit off' (meaning racist). We reminisced about the people we had left behind and wondered what our classmates in Manipal were up to. We talked about people we knew and filled in the blanks for each other about those less well known. Our scholarship included a monthly stipend and we shared advice on how to make it last until the end of the month. I omitted to mention that I had access to Papa's credit card.

They also made travel plans and each had a list of places they planned to see while we were in Germany. Their lists were endless, including places such as Paris, Warsaw, Amsterdam, Prague, Budapest and Venice. The university had planned a trip to Amsterdam for the exchange students within the first couple of weeks of our arrival and my friends decided to go on this trip. I really wanted to join them and after I returned to my room that evening, I asked Papa if I could go. His response was to the point. 'Why?'

Why did I want to go to Amsterdam? Why did I want to push my luck? Why could I not stay within my limits? Why was I never grateful for what I already had? I spent the weekend of the Amsterdam trip holed up in my room, missing my friends. I had come to rely on this group for emotional support and their presence helped me feel less alone in a foreign country. With them gone, I had a chance to reflect on how I was going to spend my time in Germany. I knew immediately that I did not want to spend it in my room. Their plans and desires fuelled mine. Why couldn't wanting to see Amsterdam be reason enough? I made a list of places I wanted to visit. I surprised myself by leaving Amsterdam off the list.

The next morning, I looked up other trips the university had organised for international students. There was a trip to Berlin coming up, with travel and accommodation all arranged for us. During the day, the bus that would drive us there from Bremen would also take us to popular sights, and at night we would be left to explore the city on our own. This time I did not ask my father's permission. In fact, I did not even tell him until the trip was just a few days away.

I had never heard Papa so angry before. 'How could you?' he spluttered over the crackling phone line. How. Could. You. I was scared but stuck to my decision to see Berlin. I understood that my parents were worried about my safety and that these restrictions were in place for my own good. After years of believing this to be the absolute truth, I was convinced something bad would happen to me if I lied to them or hid things from them. While in Manipal, I did not resent this policing because I had no desire to go on holidays with my friends and spend weekends in beach towns watching them get drunk. Manipal had also overwhelmed me and I worried about my personal safety in India. I did not have time to process my thoughts, feelings and desires.

But in Germany I had all this and more. And I wanted to explore this part of the world. It was new to me and I did not feel unsafe here. I knew I had to be careful and alert but the possible dangers of travelling in Europe did not fill me with the fear I felt when travelling on my own in India. I tried to explain this to Papa. I assured him that I would message him often, that I would let him know where I was and that I would be in my hotel room before nightfall. I told him I would have an early dinner in my room and not stray out in the evenings. I pleaded for him to understand. Then I gave up.

On the day of my trip, I got on the bus and promised myself to enjoy my first trip to Berlin. The journey there was fun, and I got to know some more of the other exchange students. We discussed our home countries and a lot of the students were interested in India and asked me questions. On the bus was another student from India who overheard me answering some of the questions about our country. He was not one of the four from my college.

The girl sitting beside me was keen to travel to India and asked me about sights to see, places to stay and things to be aware of. I mentioned that it was not always safe to travel on your own as a woman and suggested that she visit India with a group of friends. This enraged the other Indian student and he interrupted me to announce that India was one of the safest places in the world. He said he knew this because he had lots of female family members and he had never heard them complain about it. I did not react.

Later, when we got off the bus, he pulled me aside and asked me not to say anything bad about India because it made me look unpatriotic. He told me that we should resolve our country's problems among ourselves and that there was no reason to publicise them. He ended his spiel by explaining the economics of tourism and asking me if I wanted to cause the downfall of my country.

On this Berlin trip, Papa called often, sometimes every hour. His fear was infecting me and it became difficult for me to be present and take in this new city when I was being constantly interrupted. What was even more annoying was that we had nothing left to speak about and the phone calls were starting to get awkward. After freshening up in the hotel, a small group of us went to a marketplace with shops. While I was browsing in a shop that sold glass jewellery, Papa called again, probably for the fourth time that day. I decided to ignore him. This only made him call me repeatedly.

I let my phone ring as I gathered myself. I took a deep breath and focused on a beautiful, aquamarine, teardrop-shaped glass locket. When I finally took his call, I asked him in a clear, calm voice what he wanted. He wanted me to tell him (again) about the hotel and the area where we were staying and the girl I was sharing my room with.

'I emailed all this to you yesterday.' I tried to keep the annoyance out of my voice.

'What about the phone numbers of your friends?' he asked.

'They haven't changed since I lasted texted them to you.'

'Where are you now?'

'I'm in a shop, with my friends.'

'When will you get back to your room?'

'In a few hours. I am with my friends and can't speak to you right now.'

This didn't go down well. He raised his voice and told me that I would talk to him when he wanted me to talk to him. I listened for a bit and then I hung up and switched off my phone. I continued staring at the teardrop locket as I fumbled with my jacket pocket to slip the phone in. Over the course of the conversation, the teardrop had become a smudge as my eyes filled with tears, but after ending the call, I regained my clarity.

That day marked a big change in my life. I fell in love with Berlin and visited it four more times. I ventured out on my own and visited art galleries. I touched the remnants of the Berlin Wall. I stood outside the building from which Michael Jackson had dangled his child; it had been less than two years since his death. I couldn't stop my tears at the Jewish Museum. A security guard handed me a tissue and lightly touched my elbow.

Until I arrived in Germany, my aim in life had always been to please my parents. I had sought their approval and tried to make peace with our community's expectations. Leaving home and learning about other people in different parts of the world helped me find myself. Books and travel made me empathetic towards others and helped me realise that there was more to life than pleasing people. I knew that my love and respect for my parents would never change, but I also knew that I could no longer put my life on hold, just to seek their approval.

I also realised that the restrictions placed on me were not only about my safety, but also about power. I had fought with Mama all my life because of this power and I remained subservient when it came to the power Papa exerted over me.

All this changed that day in Berlin. I realised his words that day were coming from a place of anger, not concern. How dare I disobey him? For the first time, I did not feel a desperate need to be back in his good graces. I needed space and maybe he did too.

Now, when we look back at my time in Germany, he likes to be recognised for 'letting me go'. 'No other father would have done that,' he boasts. Even in this acceptance, there is acknowledgement of the power that men have over women in my culture.

Even though my father was against me travelling abroad at first, the truth is that I did it on his money. He said many things to try to dissuade me, but he never blocked the credit card that was linked to his account. At every turn in our journey as father and daughter, he allowed himself initial outbursts but always found a way to make peace with my need to be independent. This was not the experience of most of my friends with their fathers.

When I returned from Berlin and things had cooled between us, Papa shared his own experiences of travelling to Germany in the late 1980s. He talked about the sights he saw and the people he met. He shared his views and concerns. I learned of his deep respect for Germany and the way the country worked hard to improve itself after the wall fell. He made sure I had everything I needed.

A week after I returned from Berlin, I forgot my bag on the tram. I was on the phone to a friend and only realised my mistake after I had stepped off. Before leaving me in Bremen, Papa had given me €500 in cash and asked me to open a bank account first chance I had. I had been procrastinating and was finally on my way to the bank when I forgot my bag. Along with the €500 was money my grandparents had given me before I left India. They had thoughtfully converted rupees to euros, making the sum total in my wallet that day around €800.

In my panic, I called my father. He was in a meeting at his office in Jeddah but stepped out to take my call. I was crying, trying to get the words out. He calmed me down and asked if my passport was in my bag. I said I had left it in the room.

'That's great,' he said. 'You have nothing to worry about.'

'What about the money?' I asked.

'It's okay,' he said. He had to get back to the meeting but assured me that he would figure something out. He did not use my carelessness against me nor did he point out that I would never have been in this position if I had not left home.

He called again after the meeting to ask me if I had made it to my room. He told me to report the loss at the police station. He also contacted a friend who had a sister in Berlin and who in turn had family in Bremen. He requested that this family friend visit me at my accommodation and give me €200 to keep me going while he sent me a new credit card.

Losing the money was a huge setback for me in that first month. The incident made me question my decision to move away from home. Maybe I was not cut out for this after all? What if my family was right in thinking that young women are not designed to live independently? If Papa had asked me to come back home that day, I would not have protested. Instead, he told me that I was doing great in a new country and should not blame myself for mistakes that could happen to anyone.

My German friends had no reason to believe that I would not get my possessions back. Their confidence in their city's police and transport system as well as their fellow citizens astonished me. When I told them about the €800, they were less sure, giving me a look that seemed to ask, 'Why are you testing us like this?'

I was nervous when I went to the police station and all the words I had practised in German escaped me when a police officer asked me why I was there. Luckily, he spoke English and led me into his office to help me file a report. He explained that my best option would be to keep checking the official lost and found website of the public transport company.

I checked the website every day, sometimes more than once. On the third day, I found a string of words that looked familiar. *Tasche. Handschuhe. Zwei Bücher. Damen Geldbörse*. I knew this was my bag. I checked the address online and rushed out to claim it.

At the office, a man behind the till took the description down and handed the bag over. He asked me to check if everything was in order before I left the premises. The fact that my bag had made it back to me was a miracle and until that moment, I had not dared to imagine I would also get all my money back. I opened my wallet and sure enough, it was empty. Papa's now blocked credit card was there as well as my IDs but no money. Instead, there was a note sticking out of the pocket where the cash used to be. It was a receipt. I did not understand the words, but I recognised '€800'. I asked the man behind the till what this meant. 'Ah, ja, it's not safe here so we put your money in . . . ah, a bank,' he explained.

I rushed to the address the man gave me. It was not a bank but an information centre. The people behind the counter examined the receipt, established my identity and handed me crisp notes, which I took straight to the bank.

My German friends were smug for a long time after that, happy that their city had come through for me and gently mocking my lack of faith in the 'German way'. I think they were as relieved as I was.

Not knowing the language of the city slowed me down in the most unexpected ways. In India, I was able to speak to everyone in my college but in Bremen, only a small section of the students spoke conversational English. The city too felt muted, as I walked through it without understanding the conversations around me. No amount of copious note-taking in my German class could prepare me for conversations with native speakers.

I found solace in the museums, where luckily for me, all the labels and descriptions were translated into English. I enjoyed the art galleries by the River Weser, which I walked along, and I visited cathedrals. I learned to be in my own company. I felt the full pressure of being at a crossroads in my life and I was intent on making conscious choices on what to do next.

I wanted to experience everything I could. I attended my first concert, a visiting jazz band at a café. I went on my own, sat near the front, and stayed transfixed from start to finish. I did not make small talk, I did not move to get a drink, I did not keep track of time, instead I let the music speak to me. Soon, I was looking up jazz concerts around the city and going to more and more of them. One band performed on a boat under a moonlit sky. It was magical.

After classes finished for the day, I put on my headphones and walked around Bremen. I saw a lot of suburban Bremen this way. Through music, I discovered another way of understanding myself. I revisited the Indian music from my childhood. Papa is a great singer and we were often subjected to songs from the 1970s that he enjoyed. One of the songs that he sang went, *Kuch toh log kahenge, logon ka kaam hai kehna* ('People will always say something, it's their job to say something'). The actions of my community are so often motivated by the phrase, *Log kya kahenge?* (What will people say?). Being away from home gave me the courage to confront this truth about my community and decide how my values could fit in with their expectations.

*   *   *

A few months after my move to Bremen, Papa visited Germany on one of his business trips. He had work in Frankfurt and we decided to meet there. It felt good to see him after months of being in an alien city. He came laden with my favourite foods from Jeddah and wanted to hear everything about my time in Bremen so far. He asked me lots of questions and listened intently. He wanted to know about my travel plans. I had booked a trip to Venice, made plans to go to Prague with a group of girls and on another trip to Berlin before the end of the month. Papa was pleased for me and commented on how well I was doing with my newfound freedom. 'I am so proud to see you adjust so well to a new place,' he said.

On our second day in Frankfurt, he met with an old friend, taking me with him. They knew each other from Saudi Arabia, though his friend had left for Germany years before I was born. But before they began walking down memory lane, the man turned to me and said, '*Beta*, my niece is coming to pick you up in a few minutes. She will show you around Frankfurt. This way you can spend your day with someone interesting and not be bored by us old men.' I was touched by his thoughtfulness. I got ready in a hurry and before I left, Papa found a private moment to tell me not to discuss religion with his friend's niece. Papa had never instructed me like this before and I was curious to know why.

I waited in the lobby for Papa's friend's niece to arrive. Two young women in hijabs turned up and asked for me. One of them was pushing a buggy. The niece introduced herself and her sister-in-law, explaining that her sister-in-law was free for the day and wanted to join us. The sister-in-law's baby was just a couple of months old.

I was not sure what to expect from the day. All three of us were shy but I felt comfortable in their company. I had a list of things I wanted to see in Frankfurt and they were happy to go along with it. I still feel guilty for inflicting Dalí on them, but they took it in their stride. The niece was also an avid reader and introduced me to both Goethe and Kafka's work in one afternoon. After a tour of Goethe's house, we went to Hugendubel bookshop to buy copies of *The Sorrows of Young Werther* and a short story collection by Kafka. It had been a while since my last time in a bookshop this size and I kept them waiting as I browsed their large collection of English books and ended up buying more than I should have. When I turned to my new friend and made an apologetic face, she smiled and told me that knowledge is *sadaqah* and I should never apologise for pursuing knowledge.

Knowledge is *sadaqah*. What a beautiful thought. I had known *sadaqah* to be an act of charity. For me, it was about giving money to the poor and being kind to them. She explained that *sadaqah* is every kind of goodness you can do in the name of Allah. I remembered my promise to Papa and did not ask more questions.

It was an unusually sunny day and after the bookshop, we bought ice creams and sat by the river. My new friend asked me how life in Saudi Arabia was. I told her that I liked it, that I missed home, but that the place was too strict for me. 'Oh yes, the Wahabis,' she nodded in understanding. At this comment, her sister-in-law gave her a warning look and she quickly changed the subject. It seemed I was not the only one who had been instructed to stay away from the subject of religion.

At dinner with my father that evening, I asked him why he told me not to discuss religion with his friend's niece. He explained that he did not want me to say anything offensive. 'I've been away from Muslims only a couple of years, you know?' I joked. He said it was not about that. He explained that his friend was an Ahmadi Muslim. 'They have been through a lot as a community. I didn't want you to say something ignorant,' he said.

I had never heard of the Ahmadiyya Muslim community before. I was surprised to learn that this religious movement was founded in Punjab as recently as the late nineteenth century. I studied their beliefs with interest and was stunned to learn about their persecution at the hands of other Muslims. Though they are considered Muslims in India by law, the top Islamic institutions of the country had declared them non-Muslims. They did not fare much better in Indonesia or Pakistan, where the largest population of Ahmadi Muslims live. Pakistan is the only state that has officially declared the Ahmadi Muslims as non-Muslims. The main reason for this persecution is that, unlike other Muslims, they do not consider Muhammad to be the last prophet of Islam. This thinking goes against my core beliefs too, but I could not understand why this was reason enough to discriminate against them.

By the end of my time in Bremen, I had visited Hamburg, Berlin and other German cities, while also travelling to Italy, the Czech Republic, France, Denmark, Sweden, Austria, Belgium and Switzerland. I travelled on my own and sometimes with friends. I stayed in shared hostel rooms with up to twelve people. I learned to trust my instincts and overcome my fears. For as long as I could remember, I was taught that bad things would happen to me if I didn't stay close to my parents. At first, travelling on my own did feel like I was testing my luck. Every time I planned a trip, I had to overcome this fear. I understood the consequences, but I couldn't let this fear grip me any longer.

In Jeddah and Manipal, I was passive. There was a lot happening around me and there were so many people trying to influence my thinking. Amidst this, I did not get much time to find myself, to ask what I wanted from life. Away from home and family, away from those whom I considered 'my' people, I had a chance to get to know myself, my hopes and desires, my barriers and my boundaries. Bremen was the perfect place for this journey of self-discovery.

Bremen's social and liberal leanings made me confront some of my own biases against Europeans. In the East, westerners are considered to be without morals. People who gave up religion for capitalism, people who do not enjoy strong family relationships, people who divorce easily and do not respect the institution of marriage. The general rhetoric was to be suspicious of 'them', to always remember our roots and to hold on to our spiritual pasts. I was happy to have all these myths dispelled. I met Catholics who were more serious about their religion than I was about mine. I met young people who were preparing to get married and build a life with their partners. I met people who cared about the environment and those who had travelled extensively around India and had seen more of my country than I had.

I became close to a girl from America who, when I met her, was a staunch Republican and a practising Christian who had been on international missionary projects. She was also on an exchange semester in Bremen and I loved how unapologetic she was about her faith in a student environment that did not place much importance on such things. We were the only two students in the programme that year who did not drink alcohol and who wanted to travel the continent without being stuck with people with different interests. We ended up going on a few trips together and I remember how grateful I was for her company. I enjoyed learning about her family and listening to her talk about her God. She had such clear ideas about her faith and was not bothered by those who questioned it. And she never made me feel uncomfortable about my own faith. I wanted to be like that.

I learned from her that confidence comes from knowledge. She was unperturbed by other people's words because she knew her religious history and she understood when someone was mistaken. This was what I was lacking. I did not know enough about Islam to stand up for it in an unfriendly discussion. I decided to change that. I started by reading about the basic principles. I revisited the concept of *sadaqah* and other things about Islam that I was not taught at school or at home. I learned about the mercy of God. I learned about the importance of accountability in my religion and doing what we feel is right.

While my identity as a Muslim sometimes made me feel like an outsider, in India I had nonetheless come to enjoy a confidence that was unique to being in my own country. This was stripped away from me almost immediately after leaving. With the loss of language, and cultural references, I lost some of my confidence in myself. In Bremen, I was not Zeba, I was the Indian girl, often mistaken for the other female Indian student at the university. This unexpected shift made me question my identity and the importance I placed in others' perception of me. I had to ask myself what it meant to be an Indian in Europe and how my identity as a Muslim woman would fit within the narrow confines of how the West perceived women of colour.

This came in handy because many Germans were intrigued by Islam and they had a lot of questions. I did not mind the open curiosity, but I became wary of those who thought they had figured me out and wanted me to confirm their biases. There was one student in particular who began conversations not with a greeting, but with questions like, 'Why do you Muslims like to blow things up?' or, 'How can you believe in women's rights while being a Muslim?' I answered his questions with as much patience as I could muster. I did not know then that I did not owe him an answer. His white male entitlement was so new to me that I believed in it as much as he did.

For months after I left Bremen he would message me clips of terrorists and ask me to justify their actions. I kept telling him that Islam is a peaceful religion and that these terrorists are going against the basic teachings, making them non-Muslims. It took me two more years before I blocked him. By then, Britain had hardened me against Islamophobia.

My childhood was steeped in Islam and for seventeen years, this was the only truth I knew. I went to Makkah as often as twice a month and I prayed when I was asked to. I learned about the Prophet's life from the perspective of religious scholars. I listened to sermons on women's bodies and I sat through every reiteration of, 'A Muslim woman's duty is to marry and bear children'. As a child, I did not question any of this. As a teenager, if I found myself disagreeing, I tried to get rid of the thoughts. I didn't want to be the one questioning the will of Allah. I did not have first-hand knowledge and everything I knew about Islam came from parents, teachers, and religious scholars with a misogynistic agenda.

Religion was used to control the youth and 'Do not question Allah' became synonymous with 'Do not question your parents'. Unlearning this was probably one of the toughest things I had to do. My culture perpetuated other forms of harmful thinking, including, 'Unmarried women are a burden on their parents'. In my quest to give my life some meaning, I didn't want to become a burden on my parents. I was only just discovering the world and my place within it. It felt unfair to give up my newfound agency to perform the highly gendered role of wife, daughter-in-law and mother within a toxic patriarchal environment.

A part of me also understood that I had to become financially independent if I did not want to be emotionally blackmailed into a choice that was not mine. At the time, I felt my life could only go two ways. I could move back in with my parents and wait to get married. Or I could focus on building a career and becoming financially independent. I knew I couldn't do the latter in India because of the kinds of people who surrounded my family. In Saudi Arabia, with the male guardianship laws, any sense of independence was an illusion.

My semester in Germany was also my final semester and so at the end of it, I would be a graduate. There was not enough time to decide what I ultimately wanted to do. I only knew that I wanted to be able to stand up for my happiness and not get bullied into life choices that only fit my community's understanding of what women should be doing.

I knew that what had freed my mind was the distance from my community. The only reason I was even able to ask these questions was because I was existing outside of it for the first time. I wanted to make this distance last long enough to figure out what I wanted in life. It was with this in mind that I applied for an MA in Publishing at Anglia Ruskin University in Cambridge. I was offered a conditional place, which I accepted while in Bremen. I informed my parents about my decision to study further. There wasn't much resistance. I knew my parents were keen to get me married but as things currently stood with my hair, they were struggling to find a match for me. They believed that a couple more years would be just enough time to find an appropriate life partner for me.

I returned from Bremen a new person. Being away had unconstrained me in ways that I did not know were possible. I held on to these feelings and promised myself to continue working on myself and my faith. My final semester was now behind me and I was looking forward to graduating. My grades helped me secure my place at Anglia Ruskin University in Cambridge and I was all set to start my MA in January 2012. I stayed in Jeddah for four months, leading up to this date.

When Papa told me that there was no need to study abroad, I did not fight it. I knew my place, I knew what the future held. All my life I complained to Mama that she did not care for my happiness and that she did not let me do what I wanted to do. Now that she had, I wasn't sure what to do with the bitterness I was nurturing within me.

Even though this is never acknowledged in our family, it was Mama who pushed Papa to let me finish my BA in Germany. This was unprecedented, and I thought it would be the start of a new relationship with Mama. But when I came back to Jeddah after my time away, I felt that nothing had changed. The woman who went against the norms of our community was nowhere to be found. It's only upon reflection that I realise that Mama was not only battling her community for my freedom but also herself. How does one come to terms with the fact that what was perfect for her was not good enough for her daughter?

I was brimming with a sense of self-assurance that I had not previously possessed. I felt at peace with myself and finally ready to face whatever it was that had been festering between me and Mama. With this in mind, I forgot to put my guard up when re-entering my patriarchal community. I forgot to protect myself from Mama's anxiety towards my future. Mama had never said anything explicitly about my marriage but that was about to change.

While I was away, my grandparents had received a marriage proposal for me from one of their friends. Papa had decided the match was not for me and wanted to end the discussion there. But Mama could not let it go.

I had been home a few days and spent most of this time talking to my family about my travels, the sights I saw, the different people I met, the kind of person I aspired to be. My siblings were indulgent of my stories and Papa listened too. For the first time, I was the one who had come home with stories. Mama remained unmoved.

One evening, when I was helping Mama in the kitchen and talking about the cafeteria food I ate in Bremen, she interrupted me. I was standing by the stove, stirring a pot of curry. She was by the sink, washing dishes. She wiped her hands on a towel that hung from the oven door handle and took the spatula from me. As she stirred, she said, 'I want to talk to you.' Mama wasn't one for preludes. I stopped talking and listened.

'You got a *rishta*,' she said. A marriage proposal. I waited for her to say something more, unsure how to respond. She then told me who the man was. I could not believe that she thought this was a good idea. He was in his thirties and someone I had seen around the house growing up.

'I thought he would make a good husband. He has a few properties and with your hair problem, you probably should not be too picky.' I felt the world slip away from me.

All my life, I knew that my hair loss was a liability for Mama and while I struggled with the day-to-day experiences that came with it, I also struggled with having to witness Mama's disappointment in my flaws. The community we lived in was unforgiving towards non-conformers, the misfits, the unusual, whether in their looks or their thoughts. I knew this. But that evening was the first time Mama said it out loud. Before this moment, she had never once told me that I was not enough, that I should settle. We had our differences when I was growing up, but even during our worst fights, Mama always made sure I knew how special I was to her. I nodded, said something about needing a shower and walked out of the kitchen.

I remember adjusting the water to scalding hot and letting

it burn my skin because I needed to feel something other than the shrapnel left from my mother's words. I cried for a long time, wiped my red body down and put on a fresh pair of pyjamas. I had dinner with my family and excused myself early. I got into bed and cried some more. I wanted to believe I was enough, but my own mother did not think so. All those positive feelings I was carrying from the last few months left my body.

Hours later, after everyone was asleep, Mama tiptoed into my room and sat on my bed, in the dark. I pretended to be asleep. She whispered my name and I stayed still. 'Zeba, I'm sorry, *beta*,' she said. 'I did not mean it like that. I worry about you so much. I love you, I am sorry.' I did not move. I knew she had been crying too. She patted my head, pulled the duvet to my chin, stood up and watched me for some time before slowly closing the door behind her.

When I recounted this memory to a friend, she was upset for me but also wondered how much Mama has made me a part of herself, mentally, so that Mama felt that belittling me was only as bad as belittling herself. Mama had seen more of the world and knew something about it that I did not. Her desperation came from first-hand knowledge of how far our community could go to hurt me. She had seen too many young girls' lives ruined because they could not find a husband. I knew she felt as if she was doing her best, but that did not stop the hurt from seeping into my bones. The night my mother came to say sorry, I did not pretend to be asleep out of spite; I just did not know that I had another choice. That I could turn over, hold her hand and accept her apology.

A lot had changed in Jeddah while I was away and I used this time at home to catch up with the friends I had left behind. Some were visiting from America and Europe where they were studying, between semesters themselves. Some had already graduated and were in Jeddah while they figured out what to do next. A considerable number of my female friends had settled into married life and motherhood. Mama spoke highly of my married friends, as though their marital status made them better people. Even girls she had not thought much of when we were in school were suddenly 'good girls' who did the right thing.

I also met friends who were stuck in limbo, distance learning and dreaming of a better future. Right after our A Levels, one of my friends was told by her family that she could study in Canada if she saved enough to pay her own way through university. She chose Canada because she had some family there and hoped that this connection would convince her parents to let her go. She worked hard and saved money for three years, enough to see her through the first year. Her plan was to start university and then get a part-time job to help her pay her way to the end. We were getting excited about her future.

One evening, while I was in the midst of packing for Cambridge, I got a text from her. I called her right away and asked her if everything was fine. 'Yes,' she said, 'everything is fine but I will not be going to Canada after all.'

When her parents found out how close she was to achieving her dream to study abroad, they asked her how she could even think of putting her own education before her younger brother's and demanded that her savings be used to educate him instead. They said that their son had a moral duty to take care of his future family whereas my friend could rely on the good graces of her future husband.

My friend's voice was steady and without any emotion while I struggled to speak through my anger. 'But . . . how could they? *How?*'

She did not let on how she really felt. 'Anyway, enough about me, what are you up to?' she asked.

I took the hint and changed the subject. It's been eight years since this conversation and she is still in Jeddah, living with her parents, hoping to study in Canada. The last time I heard from her, her parents had told her that she could go wherever she wanted if she got married first. It's been years but I'm still not over the unfairness of how things turned out for my friend.

When I left for Cambridge, it felt like I was escaping this unfairness. Again. I felt grateful for this chance. This was the third time my parents were letting me go and I was aware of how lucky I was to belong to a family that loved me and treated me like a human being with feelings, despite my gender. A family that cared; something so basic, but so rare. This was mostly thanks to Mama, who was starting to stand up for herself, and hence her children. Papa was not a mean-spirited man, but he did not see anything wrong with his upbringing. In my early twenties, this began to bother me. I needed my father, my first ally, to understand me.

Part Four

Cambridge, Cheltenham and Reading

I moved to Cambridge at the beginning of 2012 to start my MA in Publishing at Anglia Ruskin University. It was a déjà vu moment when Papa helped me take my bags up to my student accommodation. My room here was much bigger than the one in Bremen and this seemed to make him happy. He stayed for a couple of days and we spent this time walking around Cambridge town centre and discovering the perfectly manicured courtyards and beautiful architecture of the Cambridge colleges. The place was breathtaking, and I remember both of us being in awe of what we saw around us.

Cambridge was everything I hoped for and it was liberating to be around people whose language I understood. I loved my tiny university on the wrong side of Parker's Piece but I couldn't get enough of the prestigious Cambridge colleges on the other side of the park. I often saw groups of Cambridge University students walking in robes, on their way to attending formal dinners. This used to remind me of Harry Potter and my childhood dream to study at Hogwarts.

During those first months, I spent most of my time with other international students, mostly mainland Europeans, and did not manage to make many British friends. With two evening classes each week, the MA was designed for part-time students, most of whom would hurry back to their real-life responsibilities as soon as class finished.

The course at Anglia Ruskin was one of a kind at the time and the course leaders were innovative in their teaching approaches. We covered a range of subjects, including the business of publishing, the production process and creative and legal aspects of producing content. Every week they invited someone new from the industry to address us and there were various opportunities to network while I was studying. When I first met someone from HarperCollins, I was reminded of the speaker in Manipal and his threats to blacklist me from the publishing industry in India. It felt like I had already come a long way.

That first semester, I was the only brown person in my class. I didn't know then about the diversity issues this industry faced. I started at Anglia Ruskin in the middle of the academic year as part of the January intake and at first I thought I was feeling left out because I was new to the class. I soon realised that there was a distance I couldn't cross however hard I tried. I was keen to make friends within the industry but struggled to make a connection with others in my class. There was one close-knit group of publishing students who always got the best internships and seemed to make invaluable connections. When this group of students launched a book club I decided to join it in the hope of closing the distance between us.

It was at the book club that I noticed the difference in the way these British students interacted with me. I assumed it had to do with familiarity, until I noticed that they did not behave the same way with the other international student, a white American who had joined at the same time as me. It was always the small things. The way they turned away from me, ever so slightly, when I was speaking. The way they ignored my presence. The way they never made eye contact. I couldn't figure out what was happening. At first, I thought I was just too different for them, too Indian for their British sensibilities. It wasn't until I came across the definition of racial 'microaggressions' – 'brief and commonplace verbal, behav-
or environmental indignities, whether intentional or

unintentional, that communicate hostile, derogatory, or negative racial slights and insults towards people of colour' – and connected with other women of colour in the UK, that I realised that these microaggressions were not to be taken personally. This subtle racism took a while to become apparent to me; I realised that snobbery was not to be mistaken for good taste, nor was it something to aspire to. The invaluable work of the scholar and radical psychologist Guilaine Kinouani helped me put this in perspective. On her blog Race Reflections, she discusses the impact of racial microaggressions in academic and work spaces. She also stresses the importance of acknowledging these incidents and naming them for what they are.

In Bremen I found that there was an interest in my origins and my faith, but Cambridge was cosmopolitan in comparison and I didn't stand out as much. The Islamophobia too was more restrained, though it felt just as bad as the blatant verbal attacks I had experienced in the past. When I shared space with British students, I noticed certain misinformation when it came to Saudi Arabia, Islam, South Asia and even their own history. I was still trying to muster up the courage to speak up and whenever I could, I did challenge their stilted views. Because of this, the environment I spoke up in was not always welcoming. In social settings, people asked how it felt to live in Saudi Arabia. When my experiences were not the horrific kind, they asked me to be honest. They also struggled with my feminism and challenged my right to be Muslim and feminist. When I tried to explain my understanding of Islam, they were not interested. A lot of my conversations with these strangers oscillated between discussing terrorism and women's oppression, while barely pausing on theological discussions.

I constantly found myself being shut down because my lived experiences did not match their preconceived notions about places they had never visited. My experiences were being used against me and my knowledge was considered biased because of my background. I knew better than to believe this and in a steady voice, I spoke up when I felt that my point added value to the discussion.

I was not interested in engaging with ignorant people and quickly saw the value in distinguishing them from the rest. After my experience in Bremen, I was not looking to spend time talking about Islam to people who had already made up their minds about my religion. A younger version of me would have yearned for their understanding and approval, but I knew now that everyone approaches a subject from their own narrow experience (myself included) and no minds can be changed unless they are open to it.

This realisation helped me stay grounded when a few years later, the UK approached the Brexit vote. The months immediately after the vote were also difficult. The increase in racist rhetoric and attacks against people of colour and visibly Muslim women felt reminiscent of being a minority in India and Saudi Arabia. I was struck by the airtime UKIP and Nigel Farage were granted and I questioned my decision to move to the UK. In this new reality, it helped to have boundaries, as people like me increasingly became easy targets on social media and in public spaces.

While I was grappling with the subtleties of British culture, my parents were contemplating cosmetic surgery as a solution for my hair loss. Papa asked a friend, and the friend asked a friend, and this went on until they found a doctor in Singapore who was highly regarded as a specialist in hair transplant surgery. Thinking about the surgery made my hair loss feel more real and I was still in denial about the graveness of my situation. I tried to stall for as long as I could before I said yes.

It's an expensive procedure and I didn't want to appear ungrateful to my parents. I also worried that if I didn't say yes, my family would keep reminding me that I hadn't tried hard enough to solve my hair problem. Once the decision was made I was terrified, but I was hopeful too. What if the surgery was the solution to all my problems? At the end of my first semester, I packed up my dorm room and went back to Jeddah. My brother was away at university and the appointment coincided with my sister's summer break. She accompanied me and my parents to Singapore.

We travelled to Singapore together and settled into a furnished apartment. I found it disconcerting that the doctor's clinic was situated in a mall. At our first appointment Papa and Mama provided the doctor with the history of my hair loss, Mama already close to tears when recollecting it. I did not know what to make of the doctor, but I appreciated her kindness towards Mama. She had a soothing aura about her as she talked my parents through the procedure. While she did confess that she and her team had never operated on someone so young before, she nonetheless felt this might be a good option for me. I noticed that despite her optimism, she was careful not to promise us anything.

She explained that she was going to shave a patch of my hair from above my neck and insert the follicles from this patch to the top of my head where the hairs were most prominently thinning. Before Mama could interject, she assured her that the patch above my neck wouldn't be visible. From that first meeting, my parents and I assumed that I would leave the operating theatre with a full head of hair. It was an expensive operation but Papa made the payment that day. I was booked in for a twelve-hour procedure that would take place in a couple of days.

We tried to make the most of our time in Singapore. We

revisited some of our favourite tourist spots and marvelled at how much had changed in the two years since we had visited as a family for a holiday. I tried pretending that this was just another holiday, but my dread was mounting. Papa told his brothers about our visit to the doctor and they were happy for me. One of them asked me to send him a picture of myself after the surgery. It had been a few years since anyone had seen me without my bandana.

On the day of the surgery, I arrived early in the morning with Papa. The shops in the mall had not opened yet and walking through the silent hallways in the building had an eerie feel to it. One of the nurses greeted us at the entrance of the clinic. This space was a maze of tiny rooms with white walls and white furniture. There was one operating theatre and usually the doctor and her team of nurses worked on one patient at a time. Today was my day.

The nurses were all female and friendly. They wore a white uniform and communicated with each other in whispers, even when no one else was around. The nurse asked Papa to come back in twelve hours. I do not remember saying goodbye to him that morning.

Before being taken to the operating theatre, one of the nurses asked me to sit down in the doctor's office, the same room in which the doctor had met me and my parents a couple of days ago. I sat in a chair by the door and the nurse asked me to bend my neck forward. I heard a buzzing sound and before I realised what was happening, the nurse had shaved the back of my head. My stomach tightened when I saw that instead of saving my hair, she threw it in a bin beside me. I kept my head down but from the corner of my eye I could see thick strands of my hair in the white bin. My parents were expecting me to come back with these hairs stuck on my head.

I was asked to stand up and follow the nurse to the operating theatre next door. There was a big white, reclining chair in the centre of the room with enough space around it for people to walk in single file. The walls on two sides were fitted with cabinets and worktops crowded with instruments that were unfamiliar to me. The nurse asked me to sit down and said the doctor would be with me shortly. Before I could settle down, the doctor walked in with a team of nurses. I wondered how they were all going to fit into the room.

I must have looked so lost as I was still thinking about my hair in the bin. The doctor introduced me to all the nurses and they took their places around the room. Some stood behind me. One of them stood to my right. A couple more perched on the stools by the worktop and adjusted the instruments in front of them. The doctor was cheery. She made small talk and I tried not to be rude. She asked me where I was studying. She had also studied in Cambridge. We talked about punting and she mentioned that she had been a poor student. I giggled, because I thought she meant she had got poor grades. But almost instantly I realised she meant she was financially poor. I agonised over my inappropriate reaction while she explained the procedure.

Over the next few hours the doctor and the nurses would work on the shaved patch at the back of my head. They were going to carefully pull out the follicles and the nurses sitting by the edge of my chair would work with the follicles and prepare them for reinsertion on the top of my head. Over the next few months, the hope was that these follicles would grow into hair. The doctor assured me that there would be local anaesthesia. She handed me the Wi-Fi password to keep me occupied and made space on the side table for my books. She asked me to let her know when I wanted a drink or if I got hungry. Everyone in the room did all they could to make me feel comfortable.

While the team busied themselves around me, I felt like I was having an out of-body-experience. How did I end up here? What if the hair didn't grow? What if this was a waste of my parents' money? What if there were harmful side effects to this surgery? I tried to recall the conversation the doctor had had with my parents and I couldn't remember any mention of side effects. Just when I began to panic, the doctor started injecting my scalp.

I cannot remember exactly at what point I started crying but I know that I did not stop. It must have been near the beginning of the surgery. At first, they were silent tears. I tried to breathe evenly so as not to bring attention to my crying. I had never cried in front of strangers before. Eventually, the silent tears got out of control and the doctor asked if I was in pain. I said I was not. And then I was sobbing. The doctor stopped the procedure to ask me what the matter was. She tried to keep me engaged with more small talk, asking me about my life in Cambridge, my time in India and my child-hood in Jeddah. She asked me about my favourite cities in Europe. But these reminders of a life previous to this moment only made me cry harder.

The doctor changed tactics and instead of asking me questions, she shared her own stories of studying in the UK and setting up a business in Singapore. None of it worked. I just could not stop crying. I felt a nervousness enter the room. The nurses glanced at each other, unsure how to proceed.

The doctor tried to joke that no one had ever cried in this operating room before. The nurses kept bringing me water. The doctor asked if a milkshake might cheer me up. I felt like my tears were putting us behind schedule. I kept insisting that I was not in any pain, but I did not know how to explain that I was crying for myself. For all the pain that I had carried in my heart for so long. I was crying because, for the first time, I was forced to confront the reality of my hair loss. I was crying for Mama. I was crying for that moment when my family would realise that I was not coming back to them with a full head of hair but with tiny scars all over my scalp where the invisible follicles had been inserted. I was crying for the disappointment that would engulf them.

With every sob, I let go of an old ache. The procedure was uncomfortable, but it was not painful. At one point, I caught sight of a vacuum tube that was sucking up all the blood from my head. Until that moment I had naively thought this was a bloodless procedure. Realising that I was losing blood made me even more upset.

The blood and the discomfort made me question why I was in this room. For the first time, I thought to ask if my hair loss bothered me enough to be here. For most of my teens and now my twenties, I had been forced to measure myself against my marriageability. I thought distracting myself with education and a career was enough, but it seemed a part of me was still holding on to my community's ideal. This day felt as good as any to sever myself completely from any possibility of trying to fit in with my community. I didn't leave the operating room with a full head of hair, but I did resolve never to compromise on my values again.

On the long flight back to the UK, I reflected on my master's as my one chance to gain independence from both the patri-archal structures of my community, as well as my family, if needed. I put all my effort into my university work and sought internships and scholarships where I could. I turned up to networking events and I volunteered on open days.

For a long time after the surgery, I felt vulnerable and over-sensitive. I cried often and was unable to look at myself in the mirror. My scalp was painful to touch and, once the tiny incisions healed, my scalp did not regain its smoothness for another year. I struggled to wash my hair and after each time, I felt sorry for myself. Feeling ugly and unloved, I was in peak self-pity mode. Mama called every few days to ask me if the newly inserted follicles were growing baby hair. I hated having to check, building up hope and then watching it crumble.

Though my hair did not grow back, I was able to stop wearing the bandana thanks to hair fibres. After the surgery, the doctor had shown me how to use them and gave me a few months' supply to take back with me. The fibres were in powder form and clung to my existing hair to give the illusion of fullness. For the first time as an adult, I stepped out of the house without a head covering.

A month after the surgery, my best friend received a marriage proposal that was light years better than the series of proposals she had been receiving over the last couple of years. She called to tell me that this might be the one. I squealed down the phone. Like me, she was facing tremendous pressure from her family and the unsuccessful attempts at matrimony were starting to get her down. Conventionally beautiful, my friend was fair-skinned, tall, slim and had a quiet demeanour. It was surprising to me that she too was struggling to find a decent life partner.

The 'boy', who was really a man, worked in Australia. He was educated, had a good job and was what most people would consider handsome. The families were introduced by a matchmaker who charged £2000 for the introduction. When her parents' existing network of friends and relatives didn't bring up any potential husbands, her family contacted one of the many 'marriage brokers' in town. Matrimony is a thriving business in India and there are numerous places you can go to help your children find the right partner. Regardless of their age, the potential partners are always referred to as 'boy' and 'girl'.

The boy's family came to my friend's house to see her.

They were keen for the match to work and asked the boy to come back to Bangalore to meet her soon. My friend and the boy were already talking on the phone while he was still in Australia and I got regular updates. So far, no red flags. She was happy. There was talk of an engagement party in December and a summer wedding the next year.

A few days in, the phone calls with the *rishta* boy started getting weird and my friend was apprehensive about meeting him. She was not able to articulate her feelings, so I asked her to wait until she met him before deciding what to do next. When they met, he told her she was lucky that he was choosing to marry her because she would never find a husband as good as him. I told my friend that maybe he was just joking and that there was no reason to feel uneasy about this statement. The next time they met, he showed her photos on his phone of women he could have married. There were over sixty photos in an album on his phone. 'Why was he showing you that?' I asked. My friend was not sure, but she felt he was trying to boast. Later we learned they had all rejected him.

This communication continued for two weeks before my friend realised that he had oppressive tendencies. She couldn't imagine living with such a man. His ideas about marriage were ancient and his expectations of his future wife were a cause for concern. Not only did he not want her to work after they married, but he did not think she should step out of the house without him. He also demanded all her social media passwords. I was shocked and encouraged her to call it off. The families were preparing for an engagement party which was getting out of hand – what was supposed to be a small family event at my friend's home had now been moved to an event space with a guest list of over 100 people. Amidst this commotion, my friend was not sure how to break the news to her family.

When she finally gathered the courage to tell her family,

her mother was devastated and tried to change her mind. But the engagement was called off and my friend went back to focusing on her final exams for her MA. Meanwhile, I had lined up a series of internships for the second half of 2012 and was working on my master's thesis.

Because of my alien status, I was going to have to work twice as hard to prove to companies that I was worth the hassle of dealing with the Home Office. The year I arrived in the UK, the then Home Secretary Theresa May changed the laws for student visas. In the past, international students could stay on for two years after their graduation. This gave them plenty of time to find a suitable job. I was expecting a similar opportunity, but a change was enforced, which meant that I only had three months after handing in my thesis to find a job.

The pressure to find a job took over my life and I frantic-ally applied for positions across the country. I was keen to work in London but soon realised that most publishers were either unwilling to hire a non-British person or unaware of the rules on how to go about it. As it turned out, things were not going according to plan for my friend either. I had taken on a gruelling internship and lost track of her during these months. But the day I finished, I called her. She told me that the engagement was back on. I could not believe it.

'What happened?'

'Maybe he is not that bad . . .'

'That's not a good reason to marry someone. Why did you change your mind?'

'I did not.'

'Then?'

'I am tired. I just want this over with.'

During the months I was busy interning and applying for jobs, my friend's mother continued to work on her, convincing her that she would never find such a 'good boy' again. Her mother told her that if she rejected him, she would regret it for the rest of her life. My friend had changed her number to avoid his incessant phone calls and messages after she had told him that she was no longer interested. When he had not been able to get through to her, he had got in touch with her mother and complained that my friend was being unreasonable and that he liked her and was still willing to marry her. Her mother gave him her new number and the phone calls and messages started again. That's when my friend gave in and said yes.

I did not know what to say, or why this was happening to her. But it was clear that she did not want to talk about it. She asked me about my internship and how I was faring with the job hunt. I told her how stressed I was about finding a job and how scared I was of going back home because I did not want to face the pressure to get married from such close quarters. She told me I would be fine and that any company would be lucky to have me. We did not speak again until the engagement party when she sent me pictures and I responded with a string of emojis. She looked so beautiful, it made me cry.

While my friend ended 2012 with a big party, I welcomed 2013 from the bathroom floor. I was upset about my hair and I think my friend's engagement pictures had something to do with that. In a fit of frustration, I chopped off a chunk of my hair. I then stared in horror at the lopsidedness I had caused and broke down. Because of my hair problem, I had stopped seeing hairdressers. My hair was getting long and unmanageable and the surgery had not showed any results. The doctor had assured me that I would see the difference within three months but it had now been over six.

After I stopped panicking about my impromptu haircut, I carefully shortened the rest of my hair and tried to make it an equal length on both sides. I went back to wearing a bandana and realised that if I kept my hair tied in a ponytail, I could get away with the unevenness. After clearing up the mess on the bathroom floor, I looked at myself in the mirror, forced a smile and wished my reflection a happy new year.

My friend's engagement had a huge impact on me. While I was reeling from it, I too was receiving *rishtas*. Each proposal demanded that I speak to a new person and open myself up to the idea of marriage. Mama still worried about my hair and got nervous every time I spoke to someone new. I also struggled with this because I felt I had to tell them about my hair immediately and was never sure what words to use. It felt bizarre to share something so personal with a stranger. But I knew I had to be honest before things got too far.

At the beginning of 2013, Mama's sister-in-law introduced me to her friend's son. Mama was keen for this to work out and she kept checking in with me to ask if we had spoken yet. He called when I was in London, in the middle of an internship with HarperCollins. I remember thinking that this man was better than most others I had spoken to. He asked me what I wanted, and I said I wanted to be happy. He asked me what happiness meant to me and I said, 'My life right now.' He sighed. I do not think he was keen on marriage either. Before I could tell him about my hair, he said he needed to confess something. I was listening.

'I'm not an engineer; my mother just says that to people.'
'Why?'
'I don't know. I have told her not to but she doesn't stop.'
'Thanks for telling me.'
'You are welcome. I think you should concentrate on your internship, it sounds like a great opportunity.'
'Yes, it is. Thank you.'
'You take care then.'
'Oh, can I tell my mother that you are not an engineer?'
'Of course. Good luck.'

When I later told a friend about this conversation and lamented the fact that people would lie about such things when it comes to marriage my friend simply said, 'You are lucky he decided to tell you. He could just as easily have lied, and you would not have known until it was too late.' This was true. In fact, it had happened to someone in my family not too long ago. A family from America had told one of our relatives that their son was a doctor and it was only after the wedding that they found out that he was a medical secretary. The betrayal was hard-hitting, but there was nothing they could do except let their daughter accompany her new husband to America. The bride's mother cried for months after.

Before he told me about his non-engineer status, Mama was keen for this to work out because she had spoken to the boy's mother and told her about my hair, to which his mother had said, 'How can you even think this would be a problem for us? She is like our daughter. What if something like this happened after the marriage? We would not love her any less – it's just hair!'

As expected, this comforted Mama beyond words and she felt like all her prayers had finally been answered. But the woman had also lied and I was not ready to forgive her, so Mama let it go. These *rishta* boys, as they came to be known, were a mixed bag. Some felt the need to show me my rightful place as a woman and make sure that I understood that they were the best I could hope for. Most of them approached me with an understanding that I would not reject them. And then they were always surprised when I did. This surprise caused them to say unpleasant things to me.

Around this time I read Jane Austen's *Pride and Prejudice* and a line from the book stayed with me: '[Y]ou should take it into further consideration that in spite of your manifold attractions, it is by no means certain that another offer of marriage may ever be made you.' Austen's Mr Collins and the people in my life had this in common: trying to get what they want by instilling a fear of uncertainty.

Through the arranged marriage system, I met a series of unpleasant and strange men. And for the first time, I realised how the patriarchy and my culture had failed our boys. When I look back at this time in my life, I cannot believe some of the people I met. There was one person who went into great detail about frequenting sex workers and how much he enjoyed threesomes. His understanding of romantic relationships, female desire and consent were too disturbing for me to engage with. It was interesting to me that we grew up in the same community, went to the same school, hung out with the same families at weekends, yet his experiences were so different to mine. It seemed to me that the more our parents policed their daughters, the more they lost track of their sons.

Then there was a man who gave passionate speeches to large audiences about how Muslim women are forgetting their rightful place (at home) and how they need to be taught who is in charge (the man, of course). Our 'first meeting' was chaperoned by Papa and I could tell that the man had no interest in me. I couldn't wait for the evening to be over but when the man left, Papa asked me to send him a text, so he would know that I was interested. 'But I'm not,' I replied. 'Just send him a message, you need to give him a chance,' Papa said, even though we both agreed that his values were too outlandish for us.

There was one person I spoke to on the phone three times and all three times he was high. He believed that being high was the only way to be creative. My family kept pushing me to give them an answer on his suitability. When I mentioned the drugs issue to Papa, he said something along the lines of, boys will be boys. I realised then that I was expected to take all these proposals seriously, so I did.

Then there were those who were less outrageous, like the man who kept hinting that I would look so much more beautiful if I wore a hijab, and the person who just outright said that he was looking for someone who would stay in India to take care of his parents while he lived guilt-free in the UK. There was also a man who was convinced he was saving me (from what, he did not say) by agreeing to marry me. He was aghast when I said I was not interested, truly at a loss for words.

When I turned twenty-two and was still unmarried, Mama started to panic. The hair transplant surgery had shown no results and my parents now felt I was being too fussy in picking a husband. They didn't see why I would reject someone with a steady income and wondered about the importance I placed on compatibility.

The last man I spoke to had two masters' degrees, and a high-paying management job. He had Indian origins but lived in the UK. My parents thought he was perfect. I was open to this relationship until I realised the man had deep-rooted paranoia and insecurities. He was the only person I met who was insecure about my love for books. I had a strong sense of self and when he couldn't upset me, he felt it was because I had the comfort of books to rely on. That he wanted to upset me was a red flag in itself, but when I told Mama about it, she told me that men are insecure by nature and that I could always read when he was at work. The absurdity of this advice left a mark on me. When it didn't convince me, Mama assured me that once I married and had children, things would get better. I felt sorry for myself and for Mama, that she thought this was good advice and that I had to listen to it.

The man reminded me a lot of my friend's fiancé and as things were not improving for her after the engagement, I decided I was not going to take the same risks.

I never lashed out at these men, never pointed out their flaws to them. I understood that they too were victims of our culture. They sought love, but they didn't know how to sustain it. They wanted to have what their parents had and they expected their wives to be like their mothers: cajoling, unconditionally accepting of their mediocrity and cleaning up after them. The young boys in my community were learning the same things I was: women are inferior, valued for their beauty, and are required to look after men. So how dare I, a woman from their community, reject them?

Almost every time I told someone I was not interested in marrying them, their first reaction was to tell me that I was not that beautiful anyway. I found this recurrence curious among the young men from my South Asian Muslim community. They thought attacking the way I looked would hurt me most deeply and they didn't know how to react when it didn't bother me. They usually gave up when I told them that I quite liked the way I looked and didn't need them to think I was beautiful.

Investing in my sense of self and divorcing it from the perceptions of others not only kept me afloat as a teenager but it protected me from making life-altering choices from a place of insecurity. I knew my value and I wasn't going to waste my precious time enabling fragile, toxic masculinity.

While balancing the pressure from family and the fear of making regrettable, life-altering choices, I also had to keep up with the growing difficulties of finding my place in a white industry. As an outsider, I was not at first aware of publishing's lack of diversity and naively, I believed that the reason why there were so many books by white authors was because people of colour simply did not want to write books. The reality seeped through me like cold water. I knew the odds were against me as a foreign employee, but would they have been any better if I was a non-white British citizen? I realised how far down the pecking order I really was. But I had made my decision and there was no choice but to try my best.

When I submitted my master's thesis, I had three more months left in the country. I was continuing to apply to every entry-level publishing job and preparing for interviews but as my visa expiration date neared, I had to come to terms with the very real possibility that I might not find a job in the UK and that I would have to go back home. I couldn't imagine living in Jeddah. I needed a contingency plan. I asked Papa if I could do another MA, maybe in the US this time. I had come to rely on this privilege, and as expected, Papa agreed to pay for it.

Mama, much to my surprise, kept pushing me not to give up on the job hunt, even in those last couple of months. My course leader had emailed everyone in my class about a new job opportunity in Cambridge, a position at ProQuest, an information-content and technology company. When I was going through the email, Mama phoned. She had just heard about my most recent call with Papa and asked me why I was being so defeatist. 'You cannot keep studying for the rest of your life,' she said, 'and it's not fair on us to pay for another degree when we should be thinking about your siblings. You will get a job,' she assured me.

'I don't think I can do this any more,' I whimpered. I lost count of the jobs I applied for after I hit seventy-five applications. I had been to around fifteen interviews. When I made the cut, the publishers often decided they couldn't hire a non-British citizen for an entry-level job. The new rules required them to justify each international hire to the Home Office. Mama did not want to hear about it. To her, these sounded like excuses.

'There is nothing for you here,' she replied. Those words have stayed with me all these years. *There is nothing for you here*. She was right, but I did not want to be reminded of this in my moment of weakness. Before hanging up, she reiterated, 'Apply for every opportunity you get, don't live with any regrets. We will always be here.'

After she hung up, I reread the ProQuest job description and started working on my application. There was nothing to lose.

Within a few days, I received an email from ProQuest asking if I was available for an interview. I was in the library again, looking for more vacancies to apply for. In the last few months I had received several emails like this and they did not mean anything to me. I asked if they were open to hiring a non-British employee. I didn't want to waste my time any more. They replied in the affirmative and we agreed on an interview date.

When I left the library that evening, I noticed several WhatsApp messages from my friend. She had been busy with wedding preparations and we hadn't stayed in touch. It was late in India, but I called anyway.

My friend was still awake. 'I cannot do this,' she whispered. 'I know,' I whispered back. I could tell she was crying. I cried too. I told my friend to calm down. I told her that nothing could happen without her consent. I reminded her that she had the power to make this go away, she just needed to be brave. I told her to explain everything to her parents. I assured her that someone better would come along, the person she was destined to be with. I promised her that she would always have me. She agreed to get some sleep and talk to her mother the next morning.

A few weeks later I accepted my first job offer. ProQuest was an international company who regularly sponsored non-British citizens. The job paid over the threshold Theresa May had set as a visa requirement and my manager was keen for me to join their team. As expected, the visa process was arduous, but in the end my application was successful, and I was granted leave to remain until August 2015. I had just bought myself two more years.

Exactly a month after I started my new job, my friend married her fiancé. Talking to her parents had not gone as expected. Instead, her mother had accused her of rushing into this marriage and hence bringing such misfortune on herself, which she now had to face. While my friend became busy in the whirlwind of Indian wedding celebrations, I relaxed into my new life. For the first time, I was financially independent from my parents. I was paying my rent, I was working in a job I liked, and I could afford everything I needed. I was happy. The prospect of dying unmarried did not fill me with terror any more either. The fear had lost its power because this job helped me see what life could be like on my own.

My job was more technical than I was expecting, and the learning curve was steep. But unlike my student days, I did not have to work into the evenings and at weekends. Suddenly, I had free time and enough money to start travelling again. I visited London regularly, I booked weekends away in mainland Europe and started saving money to visit New York. The more I appeared to be happy in my life, the more I made my parents nervous. Mama tried hard to explain to me that life would be even better if I married. When I asked her in what way it would get better, she could not give me a satisfactory answer.

As expected, things did not improve for my friend after marriage. A couple of months later she called to tell me she was pregnant. She was scared, unsure. At first, her husband was pleased with this development. But a few weeks later, when the doctor's report came in, he accused her of cheating on him. It was an outrageous claim and an impossible one, as he worked from home and monitored my friend's every move. 'What should I do?' she wailed. She was visiting her parents that week and her husband was sending her threatening messages. He brought up her past relationships and told her that he would ruin her life. If she was not able to leave him before they married, she was definitely stuck now. I kept trying to rationalise with her, assuring her that he was not stupid enough to lose her.

And he did not. He softened when he learned that they were expecting a baby boy. The moment passed as quickly as it came and in hindsight, I wonder if he planned this charade simply to remind her that he had the power to ruin her if she was not compliant. I cannot imagine her initial rejection sat well with him and I wondered if this was his way of getting back at her. If this was true, he got what he wanted. She lived in fear of him but was adamant about making their relationship work for the sake of their unborn child.

Later, when I asked her permission to write about her life, she paused in response and then said, 'Write the shit out of it.' My friend did not usually swear and we both burst out laughing at her response. 'Write it all,' she went on, 'let people know what it feels like.'

Mama loved this friend and since her wedding she could not stop talking about her. She kept telling me how lucky my friend was to find such a handsome and educated husband and how amazing it was that they were expecting their first child. I did not have the heart to burst her bubble, so I listened to her go on about how beautiful my life would be if I stopped resisting marriage.

I had been at my job for a few months when Mama asked me why I was so adamant on ruining my future by pursuing a career.

'You were the one who asked me not to come home,' I said.

Mama denied ever saying this.

'You told me there was nothing for me there. I applied for this job because you told me not to give up.' My voice was getting higher with every word.

'I thought the job was for a year, I did not know you would use it against us like this,' she replied.

My feminist study was empowering me to stand up for myself. I no longer felt the need to explain my actions to others. But I realised that my feminism would be incomplete if it didn't include my mother. I was still seeking stories about conflicted mother–daughter relationships and I was stunned by the sheer amount of literature on the subject. I read about Vivian Gornick's lifelong antagonism with her mother and felt exhausted at the thought of carrying on like this with Mama for the rest of our lives.

In real life too, women were talking about their strained relationships. Once in a café in Cambridge, I shared a table with a fifty-three-year-old woman who was in a bad way and kept blaming her failures on her mother. I was twenty-three at the time and it felt like this woman was a ghost from my future. I decided that day that I couldn't keep reacting to Mama's words the way I do. I knew it was time to take owner-ship of my actions and to make conscious decisions which were not a reaction to Mama's words.

The same year, I watched a beautiful French film by Martin Provost on the life of Violette Leduc. I knew her as Simone de Beauvoir's friend. The film surpassed all my expectations in its exploration of beauty, queerness, feminism, insecurities and love. It included the lines, 'Ugliness in a woman is a mortal sin' and 'I shall go as I came, intact, burdened by flaws that tortured me'. What I wasn't expecting was the exploration of Violette's difficult relationship with her mother. At the beginning, when Violette was asked what made her so unbearable, she responded, 'My mother never held my hand.'

Throughout the film, Violette's character complained, cursed and belittled her mother. But near the end, when the prospect of losing her mother became real, she said, 'I hope it never happens to me, losing my mother. I couldn't go on.' Finally I found my relationship with Mama reflected in art. The frustrations and the immense love.

The first year of my working life was challenging for my family and friends back home. They wanted to know how much longer I was going to stay in Cambridge and when I planned to marry. In my community, I was the only girl who went abroad for her studies and didn't come back home after finishing. And among my unmarried friends, I was the only girl living independently and earning my own money. I had entered uncharted territory.

At the end of 2013, I visited my parents in Jeddah. It was my first time back home since starting my job and it felt good to be there. Because I was happy in my new life, people's comments about what was missing from it didn't bother me. Instead of asking about my job or my travels, they wanted to know how I was going to convince someone to marry me. I wasn't expecting much else from these people but some of my parents' friends surprised me by expressing pride in my decisions. One of Papa's friends introduced me to his colleagues as the tax payer. He wanted to drive home the fact that I was not merely a student abroad but a professional. I appreciated these moments.

On this trip, I reconnected with an old classmate and she invited me to her home for lunch. Her husband was at work and her one-year-old daughter was napping when I arrived. During the course of our conversation she revealed that she was pregnant again.

The last time I spoke to her was after her engagement over

two years ago. She had called to tell me that she was getting married. When I asked her how she knew he was the one, she told me that her father's elder brother made all the decisions in the family and he had decided that she was to marry him. They hadn't met, had barely spoken on the phone and did not know each other's interests. Nonetheless, they were engaged immediately and the wedding was a few months later.

'Aren't you scared?' I had asked her.

'My family knows what's best for me,' she had replied.

I thought it was too late to challenge this. I wished her a happy married life. I did not hear from her until now, when she heard I was in Jeddah for a few days.

We had a lot of catching up to do. I asked her where she had disappeared to after marrying. Apparently, her husband wasn't pleased with the fact that she was in touch with her male classmates from engineering college and made her deactivate her Facebook account and delete WhatsApp from her phone. I was surprised by his entitlement, but she defended him.

During lunch, she told me I should have become an engineer and that I had wasted my time with an arts degree. She was an engineer herself but had not worked a day in her life because her husband did not approve. I told her that I loved my job and couldn't imagine my life as an engineer. But she insisted, 'You could have been an architect, you were so good at sketching.' I thanked her and reiterated that I was happy. She tutted, 'What kind of happiness is that?' she asked. I could not take this conversation seriously any more. 'When did engineering become the key to happiness?' I joked. She was not amused. We ate in silence and I texted Papa to pick me up earlier than I had previously requested.

That evening, in the safety of my childhood room, I wondered what had changed between me and my classmate. It seemed that in the past, we had had room to discuss the pros and cons of the paths that lay ahead of us. But by choosing to conform, my friend had to give up the possibility of non-conformity entirely. Because how else is one supposed to make peace with the 'choices' being forced on them other than by pretending that there are no choices at all? Maybe the choices I made reminded her of something she did not want to be reminded of.

When she told me that I would make a good engineer, she wasn't thinking about me. She was simply repeating the words that were uttered mindlessly by our elders all our lives. She knew I loved books and how much I enjoyed working in publishing. She knew I was earning more than an engineer could earn in Jeddah. She knew I had the freedom to travel on my own. It felt as though our lives had diverted into different dimensions. She had turned into the woman we both hated when we were younger. I had always wondered how the patriarchy managed to live such a long life. Now I knew. That evening, I prayed for her happiness. I also prayed that she didn't lose the fight in her like her mother had.

Allies were no longer allies and the patriarchy was destroying my existing relationships. When I used to complain about our community, my friends listened and agreed. But the moment I took steps to improve my life, a lot of them didn't want to have anything to do with me. I was welcome as long as I didn't assert my freedom to choose, but when I took control of my life and spoke out about our shared experience, they denied its existence. This was upsetting at first, but I've come to accept this as my new reality.

It felt that the freedom I was enjoying came at a cost. I was losing friends and my family did not understand what I was trying to achieve. Before landing my job, people told me they were worried because my parents could not keep taking care of me forever. Now that I was managing my own finances, they told me that I was setting out for a life of

loneliness. That I was being selfish. That as a Muslim ॑
I owed my reproductive services to the *ummah*. That I ॑॑॑
be ashamed of myself for choosing this selfish life. While the
pressure to marry and have children is universally faced by
women, my community was treating me like a spinster at
twenty-three.

On my flight back to the UK, I sat next to an Indian woman
in her thirties. Like me, she had grown up in Jeddah. We
talked about our ache for our hometown and how different
our lives were now (she was undertaking postdoctoral research
in New York when we met). We talked about how we missed
Al-Baik (a local roast chicken franchise) and how beautiful
Jeddah was during Ramadan. Our conversation took many
turns before we landed on marriage.

We were both facing immense pressure from our respective
families to get married and I lamented the lack of progressive
Muslim men in my community.

'That's not my problem,' she confessed. 'My problem is
deeper.'

I waited for her to elaborate.

'My Qur'an teacher sexually abused me for years when I
was growing up. I am not ready to be in a sexual relationship,
but I do not know how to explain this to my parents.'

This was not the first or last time I heard about sexual
assault at the hands of religious teachers or even family
members. As a young adult, this was my main contention
with my culture. To me, it signified that my culture didn't
care about protecting women as much as it cared about family
'honour'. My culture restricted women from existing outside
their homes as consensual adults but didn't think to protect
them from those who had access to their homes. A woman
brought shame to the family if she had a boyfriend, but she

also brought shame to the family if she was molested by those who were meant to protect her.

On more than one occasion, I knew of girls who complained about their lecherous uncles and cousins but were asked to keep their complaints to themselves. If they were assaulted by family friends, they were expected to continue socialising with them for the rest of their lives. One of my friends tried to move back in with her parents after being battered by her husband. She came home with bruises and a limp. Her parents were sympathetic and asked her to stay as long as she needed but made it clear that she would have to go back to her husband's house eventually. They didn't want to bring dishonour to their family name and worried that her divorce might reflect badly on their younger, unmarried daughters. My friend now has three children with her abuser and the beatings haven't stopped. Her parents are still part of my family's social network and I'm required to greet them with respect whenever our paths cross.

I believed that something like this would never be allowed in the West and I thought of Europe and America as safe spaces for young girls. The rhetoric from the West was always framed to make it sound superior to the East. It was only when I read the news of Catholic priests molesting young children and the Church protecting them that I realised how deep-rooted this issue is. The problem wasn't so much my culture, but the universal reverence we placed on men of faith, and the reputation of men in general. I couldn't keep running away from these issues.

In Cambridge, the pressures to get married continued. I tried to ignore it as best as I could, not wanting to make decisions from a place of uncertainty and fear. I asked myself what I would like my future to look like and was surprised to learn

that despite what I had seen and experienced, I di
future to include a family of my own.

The marriages around me did not fill me with conn..
and I was keen to marry a person who saw me as his equal
and not as an extension of his ego. My faith did not allow
me to live with a partner outside of matrimony and so being
in a relationship meant marriage. I understood that compromise was part of every healthy relationship, but I was not
keen on sacrificing my happiness at the altar. The men my
parents were introducing me to were from within their
network of friends and acquaintances and I wondered if
maybe widening my search would help me find a man worth
loving. It was also a lot of pressure to include the family at
the beginning of these 'getting-to-know' phases and managing
their expectations along with my own. I wanted to marry a
Muslim man and continue working on my faith. But as a
friend reminded me, there was no need to stay limited to my
parents' social circle.

When I shared my predicament with one of my Cambridge
friends, she suggested I try online dating. I was not comfortable with this idea at first. I felt vulnerable at the thought of
opening myself up to complete strangers and venturing away
from my parents' relatively protective circle of friends and
relatives. But after two years of unsuccessfully trying to find
a compatible partner, I decided that I had to take this leap
of faith. After giving it some thought, I decided to give the
Muslim matrimonial websites a miss and try my luck with a
mainstream dating site instead.

The site I used gave me an option to filter the matches by
interests. The selection dwindled considerably when I filtered
out alcohol consumers, but this was the only way I could
think of that would potentially match me with Muslim men.
As expected, online dating was a turbulent experience. I hadn't
considered the emotional toll of opening up to strangers and

investing in conversations with people who didn't always see eye to eye. I tried to maintain a positive outlook and communicated earnestly with the handful who were matched with me.

Like the *rishtas*, the online crowd were a mixed bag. I made matters worse for myself by obsessing over how to reveal my hair loss to them. It became important to me that I let them know as early on in our communications as possible, so they didn't feel like I had wasted their time. All my life, I had been made to feel that no one would want to be with me because of my hair and it became important to me that I didn't mislead anyone into believing I was someone other than who I was.

After a year of unsuccessful attempts, I felt online dating was not for me after all. I was emotionally wrung out and decided to take a break from trying to find a partner and concentrate on what made me happy. I also gave myself permission to not let my parents' fears and insecurities seep into my self-esteem. I had finally saved enough money for my much-awaited trip to New York.

That's when N messaged me.

We chatted online, exchanged emails and spoke on the phone for over a month. I kept waiting for something to go wrong, for him to reveal a side that I had come to expect among men from my background, but that moment never came. Soon it was time for my trip to New York. He called me on the morning I left, and we spoke about meeting up after I got back. There were many things about N that endeared him to me, but what I remember most from those early days was the care with which he approached our conversations, even when we were strangers.

New York was everything I needed it to be. I was surprised by how familiar it was and how welcome the city made me feel. I stayed with a high-school friend and it was lovely to see her thriving in one of the most iconic cities in the world. We had both come a long way since Jeddah.

During my time in New York, I visited every place on my list. I cycled to Williamsburg and stopped at the Brooklyn Bridge to take in the view. I cried when I entered the room in which Vincent Van Gogh's *The Starry Night* was displayed. I rode the Central Park carousel because it was where Holden Caulfield watched over his little sister. I was in awe of the city's architecture. My friend caught up with me between her classes. One afternoon we sat on the steps of the Metropolitan Museum of Art and ate lunch. 'You know this is where . . .?' she asked. I nodded and laughed as I took a bite of my sandwich. She knew how much I loved *Gossip Girl*.

Throughout my time in New York, I stayed in touch with N. I shared pictures of what I saw and he talked about his life in Cheltenham, his family and his work. He was a third-generation immigrant with Indian origins. My friend teased me about him until I blushed. She commented on how she had never seen me this happy before. I reminded her that I had only known him for a month and there was plenty that could still go wrong. She chided me for being so cynical.

Our first meeting took place a few weeks after my return. We made plans to get coffee at Starbucks after I finished work for the day. N had a day off and drove to Cambridge from Cheltenham. Despite knowing better than to expect too much from this meeting, I couldn't help feeling excited. N was different from the other men I had encountered online and I wanted to know if we were compatible in person.

On our first meeting, I arrived half an hour late. Work was busy that day, and I didn't have time to go home to change. I arrived flustered. N was upstairs in an empty Starbucks, staring out of the window. I worried he might have seen me running up the street. He stood up, smiling, when he saw me. We shook hands, I apologised, he dismissed my concerns. I felt myself calm down, smile back. It was his first time in Cambridge and I offered to show him around.

We made small talk as we walked to the town centre. I showed him some of my favourite buildings and took him on a tour of a couple of colleges. The conversation flowed freely. I was touched by his honesty and by how comfortable I felt in his presence. We talked about our childhoods, my struggle to break free from my family's expectations and his parents' separation when he was twelve. When we talked about our hopes for the future, N didn't mention any expectations he had for a partner, but rather what kind of partner he'd like to be.

The Thai restaurant I wanted to take him to was shut that day and we settled on a pizza place instead. Even though I was enjoying my evening with N, a part of me couldn't stop thinking about my hair and if he would still feel the same way about me after learning about it. Over the last few weeks, I had come close to sharing this with him but kept changing my mind at the last minute. Things seemed so perfect and I didn't want it to end. But that day, I knew I couldn't put it off any longer.

We were shown to a corner table and handed menus by an enthusiastic trainee waiter. I paused for him to finish pouring water into our glasses and opening our menus for us. When he left, I looked up from the menu and told N that I needed to say something important to him. He shut his menu and placed it in front of him, all ears.

'It's about my hair,' I mumbled.

'Okay,' he nodded, encouraging me to go on.

I took a deep breath, fixed my gaze on my hands, and spoke about my hair loss as fast as I could. When I was done, I looked up. N was nodding, his face full of understanding.

Unlike others, his expression didn't change. There was no pity in his eyes and his eyes didn't flicker to my hairline. He maintained eye contact and when he realised I was done, he thanked me for sharing this with him. I expected follow-up questions, but there were none.

'I'm sorry you went through this, it sounds painful,' he responded.

'Thank you, yes, it was painful, but I'm getting over it,' I replied.

'I bet,' he smiled. 'You don't come across as a person who would let anything hold them back.'

To this day, I can't express the relief I felt that evening. Everything was the same, yet everything had changed. Just when I was starting to relax, the waiter came back with our drinks order and placed a glass of milk beside my water. I knew I hadn't been paying attention to my order earlier, but surely I hadn't ordered a glass of milk on a first date. I didn't even like milk. I looked from the glass to N and back. I thanked the waiter and just as he was leaving, N stopped him and said, 'She ordered mint tea, not milk.' When the waiter left, N turned to me, laughing. 'You were going to drink that, weren't you?' he asked.

Despite the relief I felt at N's unconditional acceptance, we almost didn't make it to a second date when I learned about how strictly his family follows gender roles. His family set-up was all too familiar to me and even though I liked him, I couldn't see myself being with a person who didn't do their own laundry. All these years of trying to find the right partner had helped me decide exactly what I wanted in life. At first N thought I was joking and when he realised I was serious, he rushed to explain that things have always worked that way in his father's home. He assured me that he was open to change when he moved out. I also wasn't sure what to make of the fact that he was still living in his childhood home.

N listened to my concerns and responded with great care and spending time with him made me confront some of my own biases. N's priorities in life were different from mine and what was possible for me was not always an option for him. He explained to me that living at home had been a practical decision and that being able to happily co-exist with family was in fact a skill worth appreciating. I had to agree. He began working when he was sixteen and didn't begrudge the fact that I hadn't joined the workforce until I was twenty-two, or that I still had access to my father's credit card. When I revealed that I didn't have a savings account, let alone any savings, I thought he took it well, considering.

Within a couple of months of meeting each other, I knew N was the one. It's a corny thing to say, but I can't explain it any other way. N must have felt the same way because four months later he proposed. He had a ring, a speech written down in a pocket notebook and by the time he went down on one knee, I was already crying. He asked me to marry him and I said yes.

My friends all knew how I felt about him and most of them were happy for me. Some worried that I was rushing into marriage because I had succumbed to pressure from my family. Others wondered if he was the right match for me. Some of my married friends who had pestered me in the past about finding a husband were surprisingly mellow about the news. One of them even went as far as taunting me, asking how many boys I had talked to before choosing a partner and whether I had gone to the UK only to find a husband. These kinds of reactions were unexpected. It was a reminder that I couldn't please everyone.

I also assumed that after all that hankering, my parents would be excited at the prospect of my engagement. But they were surprisingly resistant. I had thought my parents couldn't wait to get me married but now that I was engaged, it turned out they were the ones who needed some time to adjust. N was very gracious when Papa requested to see his CV. N's father didn't raise any objections and N was not on talking terms with his mother at that time.

N's father invited my family to his house. I asked my aunt and uncle from Newcastle if they would come with me in my parents' absence. It was the first time I was meeting N's family and I was grateful for the support. I was nervous throughout that first meeting and, as if to manifest this nervousness, my then eleven-year-old cousin spilled cola all over my father-in-law's ivory-coloured carpet.

My aunt and uncle got on well with N's family and in December Papa travelled to the UK to meet them. All of Papa's doubts were eased after he met N's father. They got on well and shared similar values and a sense of humour. When N met Papa for the first time, he was sweating through his freshly ironed shirt. I remember Papa did nothing to ease his discomfort. After the formalities were done, N slipped the ring on my finger for the second time, this time in front of the elders, without the words (his) and tears (mine) that had followed the original proposal.

Matters left our hands after this point and our families took over. My family doesn't have a tradition of long engagements, and so a date in April was picked for our wedding. A lot of my family couldn't travel to the UK for the wedding, so it was decided that we would marry in Bangalore. N's family agreed and things were set in motion.

I celebrated the new year in Jeddah and travelled with Papa to India to select my wedding dress. Mama was doing all the other shopping but did not want to take responsibility for my dress. My best friend took me under her wing to prepare me for the big day. I left all the wedding planning to my family, especially considering they were paying for it. Sometimes N and I wondered if this was all too soon, but we also knew that we didn't want to continue seeing each other only once every two weeks for a few hours. Moving in together without marrying was not an option and we both knew we didn't want this relationship to end.

While I was not second-guessing my decision to marry N, I was starting to get anxious about my hair loss and how to hide it during the wedding celebrations. The hair fibres did the everyday job of covering my scalp, but I knew they would not stand the test of Indian wedding scrutiny. Being the centre of attention was always nerve-wracking for me, but my hair made me feel even more exposed. I decided that in order to get through my wedding, I was going to need some help.

A couple of years ago, after my impromptu new year haircut, I had mustered up the courage to look for a hairdresser in Cambridge. I remembered a health and beauty salon that had individual cubicles for haircuts. I had never seen this before and the privacy gave me confidence to approach one of the hairdressers there and tell her about my hair issues.

Claire, the hairdresser I spoke to, listened carefully and responded with compassion. She never made me feel uneasy, always drew the curtain shut and made sure no one interrupted her while she was cutting my hair. The apprentice usually washed the customer's hair at the salon but Claire always washed my hair herself. I appreciated the care she took, especially because she was the first person outside my immediate family and my doctors to see me without my bandana or fibres. Despite her kindness, these visits were surrounded by anxiety.

When I told her about my engagement, she was delighted and shared the news with her colleagues who all came to the reception area to congratulate me. While I was getting what turned out to be my last haircut from her, I asked her for advice on hair extensions for my wedding day. She did not work with hair pieces herself but had heard of a person in Cambridge who did. She suggested I meet with Garry Chapman at Scruffs, another hair salon. That evening, I looked up the Scruffs' website and decided to leave Garry a message. He called me back that same evening and we spoke briefly. I explained to him that it was for my wedding day and he asked me some questions to better understand my needs.

Garry is one of those people who can make you forget all your worries. He changed the way I felt about my hair almost instantly. He went beyond even Claire's kindness and managed to make me believe that I was a beautiful woman. We had just met, but he was excited about my wedding and was confident that he could fit me with the perfect hair piece. He also talked me through my feelings about using extensions. I explained that I did not want a full wig and that even wearing hair extensions felt like cheating. I had grown up surrounded by other people's entitlement over my body and my choices. The line between my will and others' opinions had blurred over the years. He asked me who I thought I was cheating, and made me understand that wearing hair extensions was the same as wearing makeup. He made me realise that what I do with my body is just for myself, that I don't owe anyone an explanation.

The hair piece took a few weeks to prepare and when Garry put it on my head, I wanted to cry. It blended perfectly with my real hair, which was visible from underneath the piece. He left me on my own for a few minutes, and I took a selfie to send to my best friend and my parents. My parents were thrilled for me. My friend commented on how bright my smile was and how it outshone everything else, even my perfect hair. I felt grateful for this support and with my new hair piece, I felt ready to face the naysayers.

*   *   *

The wedding celebrations were spread over three locations. They began with a pre-wedding celebration in Honnavar, a *nikkah* (Muslim wedding) ceremony in Bangalore and ended with a reception in Birmingham. When the wedding date neared, I took two weeks' leave from work to go to India for the ceremonies. It had been a while since I last visited Honnavar and it was a surprise to see my childhood playground decked in wedding lights and flowers.

My last few visits to Honnavar had not been pleasant, and coming back to this home as an adult made me slightly nervous. I had come a long way from the scared, easily intimidated girl I used to be but nothing could have prepared me for being at the centre of the furore surrounding an Indian wedding. I worried about how some of my relatives would behave. For years I had practised asserting my boundaries and being a stronger person. I worried that revisiting these spaces from my past would turn me back into the person I used to be.

I arrived in Bangalore full of nervousness, but calmed down once I joined my uncle's family. My parents were already in Honnavar for the wedding preparations and one of Papa's brothers had stayed back so he and his family could travel to Honnavar with me. They lived in Malaysia and had come over for the wedding. My aunt was excited about the functions ahead and had bought me a lovely dress to wear for the ceremony in Honnavar.

We arrived in Honnavar quite late, around 10 p.m. I was tired and ready for bed, but the house was brimming with people and it was chaotic from the beginning. Before we stepped out of the car, my uncle asked me to put a scarf over my head, as was traditional for a bride-to-be. From the moment I stepped out of the car until I entered the house and sat in the living room, I was hugged and kissed by various people, some of them strangers to me. It was an infectious environment to be in and I was moved by the time and effort people had taken to celebrate me. I focused on the positive and remembered what Garry had told me.

Just when I was starting to feel comfortable with my surroundings, one of Papa's aunts began behaving strangely. Twice she tried to pull off the scarf placed on my head and many times she tried to catch me off-guard and ask about my hair. I did not know how to respond, she was not someone I was close to, and her menacing gaze scared me. At one point her daughter came into my room without knocking and found me and Mama in the middle of a conversation. She just stood there, watching us, smiling. After a moment's awkward silence, she said, 'Oh, Zeba's hair is looking nice,' and started laughing. When she left I realised that my scarf had slipped and was around my neck. I did not mind too much, I was still wearing hair fibres and no one could tell the difference. But it was jarring. And it felt so unreal that this woman, who was in her thirties and a mother of two children herself, would do something like this. Her husband was in Dubai and she lived with her mother, refusing to go back. It's only now that I wonder what kind of horrors she was facing as a single mother in that small town. Maybe making me unhappy made her feel better about her life.

Also present during these celebrations in Honnavar was a relative who always made me feel uncomfortable. On the day after the pre-wedding celebration, when I was having lunch surrounded by family at my grandfather's house, this man walked up behind me and pulled the scarf off my head in a quick motion. I was shocked and looked up. I didn't know what to say so I just stared at him, waiting for an explanation. 'I was only trying to see who it was behind the scarf,' he responded. He exuded annoyance, as though I was the insolent one for implying bad intentions. I went back to my food.

He and his wife then insisted that I visit them at their home. I told Papa that this man made me uncomfortable and that I did not want to go. At my place, all the adults seemed occupied, so I asked my sister and my cousin to come with me. They did. We were greeted warmly when we arrived and served tea. His wife asked us to move to the dining table and as I sat down, her husband came and stood behind me. This time, I came prepared, tying my scarf tightly around my head a couple of times and pinning it into place. I was aware of his presence but not sure of his next move. I took a bite of my samosa and waited. He placed his hands on my head and pressed them against my skull, checking for hair under my scarf. I continued eating as if this were normal behaviour and not a gross violation of my personal space. After he had moved his hands all over my head I excused myself to wash my hands. It was too soon to leave so I made small talk with the couple. I knew I could not break the code and speak my mind. I could not ask for an explanation and I couldn't hope for them to understand my vulnerability.

Later that night, in the privacy of my parents' room, I asked them what was the worst that could happen if I was just truthful with these people. I saw fear in my parents' faces. Mama was close to panicking and Papa looked defeated. 'They will never let you live it down,' Mama said. 'By acknowledging it, you are giving them something to latch on to.' Papa agreed. 'If this is how they act now, imagine how they will behave once they know for sure.' I knew I was not strong enough to face such backlash on this trip. I was there to get married and I didn't have the strength to fight this. I willed myself to get through the ceremonies without giving anyone the satisfaction of watching me in pain.

A day before my wedding in Bangalore, when I was getting ready for the henna ceremony, another of Papa's aunts came into my room. I had left the door open and was sorting through some of my clothes, feeling all the happiness and nerves of a bride-to-be. I was hoping for some alone time before the festivities that evening but I didn't mind her company too much. She came close to me and tried to touch my hair. I ducked, not knowing what else to do. I had on fibres, which needed hairspray to keep them in place. She was too quick for me and managed to touch my head. The hairspray must have felt unusual to her and she asked me if I had applied henna to my hair. There was a meanness about her. I realised that she had been waiting to catch me on my own and had probably failed to do so when I was in Honnavar. I wanted to scream. I wanted to cry. I wanted to smash something against the wall. Instead, I sighed and just watched her, this woman whose daughter had recently lost her husband. I tried to imagine how that pain must feel, to watch your child suffer like that in the face of death. And I told myself to walk away. I went upstairs and found one of her other daughters helping my mother with the clothes. I sat down. She smiled at me.

She said, 'Oh Zeba, now you will be married to a foreigner and gone forever.' There was love in what she said and I felt it. Just then, her mother – the person I was trying to escape – walked in and sat beside me. I couldn't relax – what if she brought up my hair in front of Mama? I knew it would hurt her tremendously. But Mama knew, she could see it in my face. We had developed a secret language around this subject, around these people. Mama said, 'It's good for her, to be away from all these people. She never had any peace here anyway, all anyone cares about is her hair.' I looked up, astonished; I didn't think she would say something like this. Not after the discussion about not giving these people something to speak about.

What was even more shocking was that this woman, who had cornered me downstairs just a few minutes ago, was acting innocent and asking, 'Hair? What hair, what's the problem?' Mama said, *'rehne do'* leave it, and continued with her work. That day I prayed for the woman's eldest born, I prayed that Allah gives her strength in her widowhood, that he protects her from the duplicitous language of her own mother.

All my life I've had to deal with people who took pleasure in making me feel uncomfortable. At first, when something terrible happened to them in return, I thought they would realise how it feels and would change their ways. But the truth is that they aren't conscious of cause and effect; no one pauses to consider the consequences of their words and their behaviour. Causing hurt has become a pattern in my community which no one is trying to break. In fact, the onus falls on the vulnerable to not feel upset by hurtful words. When I share my pain, I'm told to grow a thicker skin.

As a society, we have many ways of expressing joy, but when it comes to dark subjects, we stay away. The reason why I didn't push my parents' decision to hide my hair loss from our nosy relatives was because I knew I couldn't rely on these people to be empathetic. And maybe that's the biggest cost of hiding our vulnerabilities, that we no longer know how to be empathetic.

I have happy memories of the rest of my time in India. In Bangalore, our wedding hall was part of a resort where our family and friends were staying for the duration of the celebrations. I had a chance to meet friends I had not seen since I left Manipal. And I still couldn't believe that I was getting married, that I had found N, that this was happening to me. It was lovely to see my parents host the wedding. I was surprised by everything they had planned for us and touched by the effort it must have taken to bring it all together.

They also booked a brilliant make up artist and hair stylist duo for me. The hair stylist was great about the hair extensions and carefully styled me for the big day. Never once did she make me feel uncomfortable about it. My wedding dress was incredibly heavy, and it took me a couple of tries before I could stand up in it. I was keen to follow the tradition of wearing a *ghoonghat* over my head as a partial veil, and because of how heavy the fabric was, it took ingenuity to pin it up in a way that didn't pull at my hair.

In my family, the bride doesn't come to the wedding hall until after the *nikkah* ceremony. My father and the witnesses came to my room to ask for my consent before the wedding ceremony could begin. I then waited for the ceremony to finish and for us to be pronounced husband and wife before I walked into the hall. Essentially, it felt like I missed my own wedding. But none of that mattered when I entered the wedding hall and saw N stand up. Our eyes met for the first time as a married couple while we were across from each other in a crowded hall. It was perfect.

After our wedding reception in Birmingham, I went back to Cambridge and N left for Cheltenham. We were yet to figure out our living situation, but decided that it would be best if I moved to Cheltenham. N had grown up surrounded by family and had just started a new job. And I felt that moving him away from his support system might be too much pressure on our new marriage.

I was attached to Cambridge but had only lived there for three years and the idea of restarting in a new town did not worry me. I looked forward to living with N and getting to know his extended family. During and after the wedding functions, I had a chance to get to know some of them and I enjoyed their company. It looked like they were a close-knit family, with the children either living with their parents or close to them. Most of N's cousins were already married and had children. The family set-ups were also traditional, with women taking on full-time domestic responsibilities.

Their social life seemed to revolve around the family and the community mosque. N's father and his peers had built the mosque brick by brick when they had been N's age. Now N and some of his cousins were part of the mosque committee. The children of the family went to the mosque every weekday after school to study the Qur'an. The call for prayer could be heard in all community members' homes via a radio transmitter.

I was grateful to be accepted into this community. Everyone treated me with respect and I had no reason to complain. Despite this, I struggled to let go of all the fears I was carrying within me. Even though I knew better than to let the patriarchy dictate my life choices, when I was not careful, years of social conditioning and observations could still get the better of me.

In my social circles from childhood, I was one of the last ones to get married. Most of my friends were mothers and were part of their own little communities and over the years, had shared with me their experiences of their new homes. Our conversations were peppered with stories of how their mothers-in-law treated them and how they had to learn their own place within their new communities. One of my friends was treated like a house servant, cleaning up after everyone in the family, serving them at mealtimes and always eating after everyone had finished their meal.

Another friend was asked to leave her high-paying job after she got married. There was no room for discussion. Her parents didn't stand up for her because the family she was marrying into was wealthy and they feared they might sever relations. This friend's cousin was already married into the same family and within four years had produced three daughters. There was pressure on her to give birth to a male child. When she announced her fourth pregnancy, her mother-in-law gave her an ultimatum: this child had to be male or else she would find her son a second wife. The cousin's mother was begging people to pray that her daughter's next child was male. In India, the desire for a male child is so prevalent that the country has made it illegal to determine the sex of a foetus.

I never asked my friend if her cousin managed to give birth to a son, but I do often think about those three young girls growing up around a grandmother who doesn't want them and whose presence threatens their existence.

When I was studying in Manipal, I visited one of our family friends with my uncle. When we left their house, I told my uncle that I was shocked by the way they were treating their maid. My uncle was about to speak and then paused, as though he had changed his mind. Later I learned that the woman I had thought was their maid was actually their daughter-in-law. Apparently, the son's family was against the match because the girl came from a poor family. When the son got tired of persuading them, he secretly married her in a mosque and brought her home. The son had joined us for the meal and there was no indication from him that he was familiar with the woman who was serving us. That was the day I understood that despite the love that can exist between partners, navigating the patriarchal set-up will always be a lonely venture for women.

As part of our wedding vows, N promised me equality in our marriage. I had spent the last few years setting boundaries and making sure that I didn't fall back into what I considered the 'patriarchal trap'. He was aware of my difficult relationship with our culture and was keen to not let it subjugate me again. I promised N unconditional love and honesty. He valued open communication above all else. His parents had divorced when he was twelve and he was keen to build a family that didn't descend into bitterness.

In our new environment, N was quick to put an end to any conversation that he felt would make me uncomfortable. He stepped in when his extended family asked what I cook for him and when we planned to have children. He reminded me that I had nothing to worry about, but I still couldn't shake off this need to play my role as the daughter-in-law. N's open support for me also made me uncomfortable; I worried that his family would assume that I was manipulating him or turning him into a 'hen-pecked husband', a term liberally used against daughters-in-law in my culture.

At first, a lot of these feelings emerged from my own insecurities. As a child, if I spoke loudly or laughed too much, I was asked if this is how I would behave in front of my in-laws. If I was obedient and followed instructions, aunts would bless me with a long and happy marriage and comment on how lucky my in-laws would be to have a daughter-in-law like me.

When I was a skinny teenager, a friend's grandmother commented on how my hips did not look like they could give birth. Later, when I was at university in Germany and England, my extended family wondered out loud about my marital prospects. Now that I had left home, surely no well-respecting family would want me, they said. When I accepted my first job offer in Cambridge, I was made to feel that a greater achievement would have been to convince a man to marry me. I think, subconsciously, what I was feeling at the beginning of my marriage was gratefulness at being accepted.

After six years of living on my own, I also felt unmoored in my new surroundings. I went from living alone to inheriting a big family of numerous aunts, cousins and children who called me auntie. I enjoyed their company, but I didn't have as much time for reflection or self-compassion. I had to adjust to new traditions while trying to maintain my own sense of self. In the beginning, I couldn't manage both and found myself setting aside my beliefs to please those around me, to fit in, to feel accepted.

In all this confusion, I unwittingly prioritised being the perfect daughter-in-law over being a supportive wife. N kept his promise, but I allowed my fears to guide me. When I lived with N's family, I overheard other relatives complaining about their daughters-in-law on a regular basis. I understood that this was a common subject of discussion and I was keen to not give anyone a chance to speak about me like that.

I was failing to be a supportive wife because I was worried that people might think N had changed because of me, that I was influencing his thoughts and causing a rift with his family. This might sound like a silly fear to harbour, but this is the reality for many women I know, including Mama.

In my community, women are treated as a liability when it comes to marriage. At every step, we are reminded that we are not worthy. Every decision we make about our lives is treated with contempt, especially those that give us freedom and happiness. Parents stop their daughters from pursuing higher education because it might ruin their marriageability. They are not allowed to travel on their own lest their future husbands doubt their chastity. No one ever stops to ask why any of these things are considered a threat. I think that's because deep down we all know that an empowered woman will not tolerate mediocrity. And if women stopped tolerating mediocrity in my community, entire households would come crumbling down in days.

While this awareness is useful, it doesn't ease the difficulties of being a non-conformer within patriarchal structures. It's grim to challenge the norms when the women are nodding along. It's uncomfortable to call out casually sexist jokes when

n laugh the hardest. I don't believe that the women
conform are unaware of the undertones that dominate
patriarchal societies. In fact, I believe that they too are aware
of the oppression; it's difficult not to be. And maybe it's
because they took the easy way out – and maybe wish they
hadn't – that they resist the most when some women choose
to walk the road less travelled.

As a teenager, I was amazed by the passion with which
women enabled the patriarchy, how carefully they enforced
the rules and how bitter they became towards women who
took that leap of faith and made something of themselves
despite the community's pressures. I watched these enablers
fight tooth and nail to oppress other women. This phenom-
enon of women being women's worst enemies was a
conundrum my younger self just couldn't grasp. It was only
through my years of studying how intentions and insecurities
manifested themselves that I understood this deep-seated
bitterness.

Even after I left home, I found myself trapped within
patriarchal thinking. I had to consciously liberate myself from
it by understanding that I don't owe anyone an explanation
for how I choose to live my life. My faith helped me. My
knowledge of Islam and my feminist interpretations of my
religion stopped others from using it to oppress me. I suppose
in this way, I was not a typical daughter-in-law. But I got lucky
because N's family accepted me unconditionally. I didn't face
any of the pressures my friends faced. Even when N's family
didn't agree with me they never made me feel unwelcome or
like I didn't belong.

One of the recurring disagreements arose because I didn't
take their name when I became part of their family. One of
N's female relatives couldn't let go of this and brought it up
whenever we were alone. At first, I tried to explain my feminist reasons for keeping my name, and my rights as a Muslim

woman to do so. I discussed the culture I came from and why it was important to me that I kept my name. I made sure to let her know that I understood why women change their names and that for me it's about choice. I didn't want her to think I was judgmental about women who took their husband's name. None of these reasons seemed to stick and the topic kept coming up. The last time she brought up this subject, I simply said that I didn't want to change my name. I held her gaze, expecting some form of resistance. But there was none. I wonder if it was my freedom to choose my name that left her dumbstruck.

For the patriarchal structure to work, women can't have choices. By marrying into N's community, I was re-encountering the patriarchy. But this time, it was on my terms. In the years between leaving my family home and moving into my new family's home, I had made peace with a lot of the patriarchy's faults. After years of study and reflection, I understood why the oppressed are sometimes the most oppressive.

I use the word oppressed often when sharing the experiences of women in my community, but I wonder if the correct word is traumatised. Conforming to the patriarchy can be a traumatic experience and often women and men go along with it because they believe they don't have a choice. So when a younger person comes in, confident about their place within the family and secure in their marriage, it must surely bring up their past trauma. It probably reminds them of their own experiences as a new bride and they too might wonder why this younger daughter-in-law gets an easy ride; why shouldn't she suffer like they did?

This way of thinking comes from repressed trauma. Women might think they have forgiven their oppressors but it's only when they themselves come into some power that we realise how much these women have suffered and how difficult it is for them to forgive. Of course, oppressing the next generation because of our own terrible experience is not a valid excuse. And it's not the responsibility of the younger generation to take on the trauma of the previous generation either. While I pitied them and empathised with their situation, I knew not to let their negativity dictate the course of my life.

In communities like mine, the patriarchy is inescapable; it shapes every part of our existence regardless of our gender. I think of the patriarchy as a building, shaped like a house but, in fact, a prison. It's old and its design is not working for half the people who inhabit it. It's rigid and too strong to be clawed out of. And when you show signs of resistance, you are crushed by those who are imprisoned with you. The only way out is to stop thinking about the structure. The moment you imagine yourself to be free of it, you are. The walls come crumbling down and you realise that its true power is in your head. You then have a choice to walk away from the ruins. But then you hesitate. You have lived here for so long; will you be able to manage on your own? Will you miss the people who live within the patriarchy? The answers are yes and yes.

Getting married and becoming part of a close-knit South Asian Muslim community was a lot like walking back to the structure I had left behind. Except this time, I was prepared. I knew the tricks to unlock doors, I could discard the blue-prints and make my own way through the old house. The structure was in place, but it didn't have any power over me. Imagine living with someone whose reality is not the same as yours. Who doesn't ask the questions you ask, who is able to walk through doors that are locked for you, who is new to this space yet familiar with how everything works. I can imagine why my presence was disturbing for women who had been conforming all their lives. And I can understand why they felt the need to attack. This didn't bother me, but I had to figure out ways to survive these attacks without turning bitter myself. That's how I came to practise radical self-care.

Previously, self-care meant long baths, essential oils and three hours of bedtime reading. It meant a manicure, a massage or a trip to the theatre with a friend. It was a way to be indulgent with myself. But now radical self-care meant being aware and accountable for the spaces I occupied and the people I surrounded myself with. I knew that the vicious cycle of trauma and oppression had to end with me and to make this possible, I needed to put myself first.

My first rule of radical self-care was simple: if in doubt, detach. With people who couldn't bring themselves to share in my joy, the detachment gave me the space I needed to truly appreciate the good things in my life. Instead of spending time doubting their intentions, I learned to emotionally detach myself from the double meaning of their words. I stopped seeking approval from people who enjoyed withholding it.

I also became conscious of not letting my boundaries become barriers. It was important to me that I continue expressing myself and approaching life with honesty and earnestness. I knew that the patriarchy would win the day I made space for bitterness in my heart. Regardless of the way I was being treated, I had to remain open, I had to show people that it was possible to walk a different route and find contentment.

N had already accepted me for who I was. Ours was not a marriage that thrived on my oppression. This dynamic didn't match patriarchal expectations and it took a while for others around us to adjust to our marriage. I couldn't be scared into conforming because I was not scared of losing my husband. I loved him deeply, but I was not going to let this love compromise my dignity. I had lived on my own and I knew I could go back to that if needed. This was a choice not many women in my community have.

The South Asian Muslim community in Cheltenham is small. Everyone knows everyone and there is both a sense of community as well as pressure to conform. At family functions I became known as N's wife, rather than by my own name. People were curious about my background but not confident enough to ask me about it. I caught them watching me or talking about me but when I smiled and introduced myself, they looked away. Their behaviour reminded me of the people from Honnavar, a connection which surprised me.

This was not my only experience with the community, but at the beginning, it was the one that stood out. I went on to befriend Muslim women who were pursuing their dreams while expertly managing the expectations of their family. I met women who refused to 'settle down' in marriage and were confident enough to wait for the right person to come along, a feat that requires immense strength within a community like ours. I met women who drove across Europe to raise funds for Palestine and those who ran successful businesses. Most importantly, they did all this while staying within the boundaries of familial expectations and practising their religion in their own unique ways. They gave me the confidence to pursue my dreams and live life on my own terms without apologising for my happiness.

I understood the insecurities that engulfed the people around me, but I was no longer taking responsibility for other people's words, thoughts and actions. Throughout my childhood I meditated on others' harsh words. I wondered why Papa's family treated me the way they did, why they made me feel bad about my hair, what they got out of it. But radical self-care left no space in my head for such meditations. Now I was focused on my own words and the way I dealt with situations. I didn't overthink other people's words and instead, gathered my own and used them to put a stop to behaviour that made me uncomfortable.

Radical self-care meant putting my needs first and being selfish about my happiness. It helped me weed out people who couldn't bear my happiness. Nothing was personal, it was just how the patriarchy worked. I understood that a happy, self-content woman was an obstacle in the wheels of the patriarchy and I stopped trying to fit in.

I stopped agreeing with everything that was said and chose to speak only when I wanted to, or if I had anything of value to add to the conversation. I stopped engaging in conversations about other people in the family because it always left me feeling drained. I joined book clubs and publishing groups. I made friends outside of the community and kept myself grounded by continuing to meet community members who were kind and open.

When I was growing up in Saudi Arabia, non-conforming women were not visible. The law kept them out of the public eye or pushed them into a limited workforce. Women who wanted to break free were legally bound. In Cheltenham I noticed that it was possible to be part of a patriarchal family and still set my own boundaries. Watching young women in the community live their best lives was empowering. For the first time I realised that running away is not the only option. At least, not any more.

From being around my own family, I had learned that people did not mean to sabotage my happiness, they only meant to uphold their values. Knowing this made it easier for me to exist within the patriarchy. I knew better than to want to be understood by people whose reality was not mine. I also realised that there is no polite way to tell someone that their forced reality is not the only way to exist in this world. I had the privilege of books and education, I had experience living on my own and distancing myself from toxic values.

When I spoke to my friends after I got married, I realised that our experiences were similar but my reaction to it was different. I felt confident enough to walk away from situations that made me uncomfortable. If I was not happy with how someone spoke to me, I asked them to explain what they meant. This usually made them backtrack and behave themselves. I realised that I didn't need N to stand up for me after all, that speaking for myself was better. I asked him to stop checking in with me at family gatherings and I didn't mind being in my own company at community events.

Patriarchy expects us to play our roles, and these roles are scripted. Expressing or expecting empathy meant deviating from this script. At first, I struggled to engage with people while remaining guarded. And every time I tried to be myself, I was left with fresh wounds. I'll admit that it was not easy and I often ended up sticking to the script too, trying to avoid meanness where possible.

Taking the high road is not easy and it's without instant gratifications. One interaction on the wrong day can still unravel me and it reminds me that I'm a work in progress. That my fight is not with others but with myself. That my role within the patriarchy is not to destroy it but to make myself immune to it. That my role in bringing down the patriarchy is to be the woman who inspires hope in young girls.

When we moved to our own place in Cheltenham, we did more of what we wanted to do without worrying about how our marriage was perceived. N took to cooking occasional dinners without the fanfare that followed his activities at his father's home. Whoever needed fresh clothes did the laundry. We took turns to clean the house. N dealt with the bills and I expanded on my quick-fix dinner skills. We both enjoyed washing dishes and knew how to clear up after ourselves. For someone who was used to having everything done for him, I had expected resistance from N. When I asked him about it, he told me that his mother had raised him differently from the way other men in the community were raised.

Because of all the Indian TV dramas and real life, I had developed an unreasonable fear of mothers-in-law. It was the one thing I was nervous about when I married and, as if to prolong my agony, I did not meet my mother-in-law until two years after our wedding. By coincidence, she had moved to Saudi Arabia for work. When I finally met her, my mother-in-law enveloped me in a warm hug and I felt all my fears dissipate.

A few weeks after that, she visited us in our new home. She was coming over for the weekend and I was fretting all week, making sure the house was clean and wondering what I would cook for her. I should not have bothered because she came laden with M&S ready meals. She told me that she did not want me to worry about cooking for her and that she would rather spend the time getting to know me than have me slave in the kitchen for her. This was a new experience for me and I appreciated her efforts to make me feel comfortable and less scared of her.

The move to Cheltenham not only helped me get over my fear of the patriarchy but it also gave me a chance to be part of a community. My experiences with my own Muslim South Asian community was not what I would call a success. Integrating with N's family and community helped me overcome some of my own prejudices and biases.

In Cambridge, I had stayed away from South Asian communities and preferred to socialise with my English or European friends. This was due to my previous experience with such communities in Saudi Arabia and my extended family back in India. I felt that they couldn't respect my boundaries and it felt easier to maintain distance than to confront my biases.

In Cheltenham, I was intrigued by the journey N's grandparents had made and how their children's lives had been

by this move. I asked questions about their childhoods
…t it was like to migrate in the 1970s. I realised that
compared to them, my immigration was one of privilege and
choice. My first privilege was probably the fact that I had a
choice. I moved to the UK as an act of free will and because
of my desire to pursue a career in publishing. My in-laws and
others who migrated between the 1950s and 1970s did not
always have this privilege. Many of them did not know what
they were signing up for and most didn't make it back home,
even though they had wanted to. Some people's financial
situations made it impossible for them to afford tickets to
India and it seems a whole generation of young South Asians
grew up in the UK without the company of their ageing
parents. When I first moved to the UK, I would visit my
parents twice a year, sometimes more.

Cambridge in 2012 was also a different landscape to
Cheltenham in the 1960s. My in-laws' family migrated to a
post-war Britain in need of manual labour. British-colonised
countries were still recovering from the enormous loss of
wealth and resources at the hands of their colonisers. In the
early 1800s, a British trading company had taken advantage
of a collapsing Mughal Empire and the many minor princely
states comprising the Indian peninsula to move assets (mostly
in the form of tax) from the subcontinent to the UK. There
is a notion that is not challenged enough that the British left
India richer than they found it, that there was significant
economic growth throughout the colonial period. In 2006,
British economic historian Angus Maddison debunked this
belief in *The World Economy*. He demonstrated that at the
beginning of the eighteenth century, India's share in the world
economy was twenty-three per cent and that it dropped to
just over three per cent when the British departed in 1947.

's independence from the British Raj in 1947 was hard-
the journey that followed was harder. Partition

remains one of the largest mass migrations of humans in modern history and the estimated death toll is over two million. Two decades after its independence, India remained grimly poor. This left people with no choice but to leave their home-towns. Some moved to bigger cities like Mumbai and Delhi. Others pursued opportunities abroad that they had heard of. There were rumours of the Queen welcoming former colonial subjects because her country was in dire need of labour.

Many of the families who migrated to the UK came with the intention of earning enough money to go back home. But hardly anyone left. When I asked one of the elders why they didn't move back he said there was nothing to go back to. After their parents passed away, people stopped visiting their families and lost touch with their siblings and cousins. They have more family in the UK now and want to stay close to their children and grandchildren, who identify as British and wouldn't consider moving to South Asia. Also, the money these immigrants earned from working in foundries and food or textile factories was only just enough to pay their bills and make ends meet in the UK. Whenever they could, they sent money home to their parents. But hardly anyone earned enough to start a new life back in India. Instead, they focused their energies on giving their children better opportunities in a foreign country.

N's maternal grandfather, his Nana, migrated in the 1950s and his paternal grandfather followed in the 1960s. N's maternal grandmother, his Nani, had one sister. The sisters grew up in Mumbai at a time when there were not enough jobs in the newly independent country. As part of the dowry for both his daughters, N's great-grandfather offered his future sons-in-law tickets to England. Nani's husband took him up on the offer. I am not sure what his plans were, but he ended up running a corner shop after their move from Cheltenham to Leicester. For a long time, he suffered from bad health and passed away years before I came into the family. During his years of illness, his wife and eldest daughter (my mother-in-law) took care of the shop.

N's paternal grandfather, his Dada, arrived in February 1960. He came alone, leaving behind his wife, four daughters and a son (my father-in-law). He worked in Blackburn and eventually moved to Cheltenham. He had heard there were better job opportunities in the south. Like most others, his intention was to work for a few years in England, save enough money for his family, and move back to India. But things were more difficult than he imagined. A few years after his move, and because laws were getting strict regarding the ages at which migrants' children could legally move to the UK, he arranged for his eldest daughter to come to the UK, to work with him. She lived with her father for around four years before they could get their entire family to Cheltenham.

N's Dada mostly worked as a labourer. In Cheltenham he worked for a company that manufactured skip loaders and tipping cylinders. For a while he was at ICI, a chemical company that produced cleaning products in Gloucester. He worked as a janitor and enjoyed the night shifts.

His wife also worked after she moved to England. In India, they owned a shop and some land. They sold groceries, mostly lentils and oil. In Cheltenham, she worked at Tilley's crumpet factory and so had to adjust to working for others. Her job was to push the crumpets out of their rings. Some days she brought burnt or broken crumpets home, which her children enjoyed with a lick of butter.

My father-in-law went on to get an education in a local public school that was hostile towards him. His four sisters, N's aunts, all got jobs in factories and worked their way to retirement. These women went on to raise assertive and hard-working daughters who contribute to their society and are in turn raising a generation of British Asian children who are still facing some of the same dreadful attitudes their parents and grandparents had to deal with.

After two years of living close to family, we moved again. This was N's first time living away from his hometown and it gave us the space to further unlearn harmful, patriarchal practices and keep working on our marriage. The distance gave me perspective and my experiences made me sympathetic towards Mama. Being a daughter-in-law gave me an insight into Mama's experiences of married life. I could now imagine how much more difficult it must have been to navigate married life without the privileges I had. Fragmented memories from my early years began to fit within their proper context and I began to understand what Mama had been through just to ensure that I would have more options than she did. I realised that I was able to leave the toxic environment of my first community only because she didn't fall into the vicious trap of recycling trauma for the next generation. Instead, Mama allowed her experiences to motivate her children.

I also started going to Mama for advice. While Mama might not be experienced in job hunting, flat sharing or modern dating, she knew a lot about the kinds of people who occupied our shared community. At first, I was apprehensive about sharing my thoughts and experiences with her. I had never done this before because I thought Mama would not understand, that all she wanted for me was to marry and have children. But Mama was surprisingly robust with her advice. While she herself accepted a lot of emotional abuse from others, she was adamant that I should not. I worried that my methods of dealing with the patriarchy would make her uncomfortable, but she was supportive. Instead of pushing me to be submissive, she started practising self-care too. It felt like we were fighting our demons together. Today, I feel as free as I do only because I know Mama is free too.

Radical self-care also led me to unconditional self-love and acceptance. It helped me understand who I am and how to recognise my hopes and desires.

Self-love helped me look at myself with compassion. I took control of my relationship with my hair by deciding for myself what is acceptable and what isn't. Becoming aware of my boundaries protected me from more experiences like the hair transplant surgery. My hair loss has not improved, but my attitude towards it has. There are still days when I wake up and feel sad. The days on which I wash my hair are always unpredictable. Sometimes an accidental glimpse in the mirror when stepping out of the shower can make me cry. Occasionally I cancel plans because I can't bear to be around people. I worry they might notice the hair fibres or ask me questions about my hair. I worry that one wrong question from them would unravel me.

But instead of letting these emotions derail my sense of self, I engage with them. I ask myself why I'm feeling the way I do. I recognise that I live in a world that is constantly selling me the image of a perfect woman. I forgive myself for falling prey to these messages and I remind myself of how loved I am. It also helps that I chose a partner who doesn't see my hair loss as a flaw or something to use as leverage in our relationship, a trait that is common with men in my community.

This unconditional acceptance created a space for me to love my body and also to find my voice. Around this time, a newly formed Scottish publisher named 404 Ink asked me to write an essay for their anthology, *Nasty Women*. They wanted me to write about my experience as a Muslim woman of colour in the UK. I was surprised by this offer – I didn't think I had anything interesting to say – and almost declined. But I was reminded of what Mama always said about how opportunity shouldn't be met with hesitance but grabbed with both hands.

The essay made me reflect on my experiences of living in the UK. When I first moved here, I wasn't planning on staying long. It was only after I got married that I stopped to reconsider my surroundings and find a place for myself within this divided society.

Muslim women are a minority in India as well, but I've never seen anything quite as callous as the discussions and publicity surrounding Muslim women in the UK. The politicians too kept getting it wrong, starting with David Cameron commenting on us being 'traditionally submissive', to Boris Johnson comparing women in niqabs to letter boxes. The interest in and judgment of Muslim women's bodies was striking. It reminded me of my time in Saudi Arabia, everyone speaking for the women, but no one interested to hear what they themselves might have to say on the subject.

Europeans were curious about my time in Saudi Arabia and asked me lots of preposterous questions about the living standards of women in the country. While I understood where they were coming from, I was always taken aback by their lack of interest in similar issues within their own countries. Something about the distance between them and the East helped them digest the cruelties better, I think.

I had come to expect casual misogyny from the older generation of British men, but when young, educated, self-proclaimed liberal men spouted vile thoughts, it made me wonder if Western culture is that much different from the East when it comes to misogyny. In fact, I can safely say that in certain aspects, the East is far ahead of the West. An example is the number of women leaders in the East, something that was highlighted for me when Hillary Clinton came close to becoming the first female President of the United States. In India we elected our first female Prime Minister in 1966 and first female President in 2007. Benazir Bhutto served her first term as Pakistan's Prime Minister between 1988 and 1990. Corazon Aquino was the Philippines' first female president, serving between 1986 and 1992.

What surprised me even more was Western women's attitudes towards me. Feminism came late to me; I was twenty and living in Europe when I embraced the label. While I chose to uphold my Islamic values, I read widely from within the feminist discourse and without prejudice. When I moved to the UK I discovered non-fiction works by Gloria Steinem, Caitlin Moran, Mary Wollstonecraft and Margaret Atwood. I read the journals of Virginia Woolf, Katherine Mansfield and Susan Sontag. I identified with their struggles to carve out their own individuality and to remain themselves in a world that was keen to change them. I took what worked for me and I tried to implement these ideas in my own life.

In the UK, I joined online discussions and became vocal about my values on social media. I supported women doing important activism. I accepted their values and understood where they were coming from. But I felt that the same courtesy was not being extended towards me. At first, I thought it was because I was not British, but over time I realised it was because I was not white. It was a subtle difference and it took me time to realise that mainstream feminism did not always have space for me. Issues that impacted me and women who looked like me were not discussed as widely as 'Western' issues were. And when Muslim women were discussed, it was to blame us rather than help. The hijab and niqab were always discussed as practices forced on Muslim women, even when we talked about how it was an individual choice. Instead of focusing on our voices, it looked as though mainstream feminists were keen to create their own narrative for us. I think they liked the idea of 'saving us from ourselves'. This was reflected in the publishing industry as well, where most stories featuring Muslim women were not about empowerment but enslavement.

Disillusioned by the feminist community I thought I could rely on, I started looking for voices of colour. This way, I came across strong Black voices that helped me find my own community. I was surprised by the sheer volume of material left behind by Black women. From Kimberlé Williams Crenshaw I learned the definition of intersectionality (sexism, class oppression, gender identity and racism are interlinked) and began identifying as an intersectional feminist. I read about how Betty Friedan alienated women of colour from the second-wave feminist movement. I came across Black lesbian feminism as a political identity and felt a shift in my way of thinking after reading Audre Lorde's words. I read works by Pat Parker, Claudia Rankine and Janet Mock. I became acutely aware of the intellectual work of Black women from which intersectional feminism grew.

In my bid to find a wide range of voice, I also read books by Sara Ahmed, Ismat Chughtai, Sara Suleri and Salma. Women before me had felt similarly excluded, but instead of letting that define them, they created their own narratives. This gave me the confidence to find my feminist voice and not feel the pressure to align with the mainstream media.

My newfound identity as an intersectional feminist also gave me the courage to assert my boundaries in real life. I ignored the provocative questions from racist people I met in person and I ignored online trolls who seemed unable to digest that women like me exist.

Nasty Women's phenomenal success changed the way I felt about my experiences. Margaret Atwood and Ali Smith read the book and loved what it stood for. The anthology appeared in bookshops across the country, sitting shoulder to shoulder with books by Roxane Gay, Susie Orbach, Chimamanda Ngozi Adichie and Gloria Steinem. Seeing my words occupy such prestigious spaces gave me the confidence I needed to speak my truth. The essay reached a wider audience than I could have imagined, and it was heartening to hear from young women who had similar experiences to mine and who found solace in my words.

A couple of years after the publication of *Nasty Women*, N and I visited my family in India. We went back to Honnavar for Eid and spent some time in Sirsi. I hadn't been to Honnavar since the wedding and during this time, I had had a chance to move on from the experiences of my last visit. I met people who were insensitive about my hair and, as expected, behaved just as they did three years ago. But this time I was ready. When my grandfather's brother put his hand on my head and asked me if I had applied henna (a question his wife had asked me before), I picked up his hand by the wrist and placed it on his lap. I held his gaze for a long moment before going back to the conversation I was having with my sister. He didn't dare to try anything else.

When it was time for afternoon prayers, I excused myself to go and pray in my room. Because of how intrusive people were being, I decided to lock the door behind me before I started praying. Midway through my prayers, I heard loud noises outside the room. I finished in a hurry and opened the door to find N standing guard. Standing beside him was Papa's aunt, looking scared. N was staring her down. He knew her as the woman who was obsessed with my hair and who kept trying to corner me the last time we met. I asked him what was going on, and he said, 'I wasn't going to let her come near you.' It felt good to be protected like this; it was the only thing I ever wanted from my own family. The woman left me alone after that.

That evening, after everyone had left, Papa asked me how it felt to see everyone after so long. I told him about the incidents. Papa nodded and then changed the subject. This was not what he wanted to hear. Later that night, N commented on this. 'I can't believe your father didn't say anything, how can he let people treat you like this?' It was a question I had finally stopped asking myself.

Papa takes pride in providing for his family. When we reflect on my journey so far, he always tells me how happy he is that he could give me everything I needed to become the person I am today. I know he is referring to financial support, but the truth is that by refraining to speak up for me within his family, he pushed me to speak up for myself. Among the many privileges afforded to me as his daughter, I think this is the one that has been most life-changing. Growing up, it hurt me that he never confronted his family on my behalf. I saw this as a weakness on his part and I assumed that his silence meant he loved them more than he loved me. I wondered if I could ever forgive him for this, but I know now there is nothing to forgive.

While he might not have confronted his family for me, he didn't stop me when I stood up for myself. Most importantly, he did not let his family influence his decisions when it came to the choices I made. Despite their best efforts, he let me be. He overcame his biases and fears for my sake and I guess he pushed against his relatives in his own, subtle ways. He didn't waste his time trying to explain his decisions to them and instead concentrated on tangible ways in which he could improve my life. And in this way, he taught me to focus on the things that mattered.

I'll always admire Papa for his ability to truly forgive people. I used to wonder if this characteristic made him susceptible to bad behaviour from others. I used to worry for him. But the truth is that he is at peace with himself. I admire this about him. Of course, the fact remains that as a man within the patriarchy, there is a lot less to forgive.

Growing up, I was always made to feel I was not enough. If I hadn't had the courage to look beyond these words, I would have probably died believing this lie. I used to look for myself in books and films. I wanted to be seen, to be heard. I wanted to listen to a voice that sounded like mine. I wanted my existence to be acknowledged. I wanted someone to say that I'm beautiful just the way I am. That I don't need to let my hair loss define me. For years I yearned for love and acceptance until I realised that the voice I was looking for was mine. That it's been here all this time, and all I had to do was listen. To open myself to the possibility of becoming myself.

Acknowledgements

I want to start by thanking my editor Francine Toon for her valuable insight, immense empathy, astute advice and her patience. I am also grateful to Sophia Brown and Barbara Roby for their thoughtful and careful editorial support. And to Miranda Doyle and Nelima Begum for reading early drafts when I was most in need of a boost in confidence.

Everyone at Sceptre and Hodder who helped bring this book to life. Many thanks especially to Sarah Christie, Helen Windrath, Melis Dagoglu, Rachel Southey, Louise Court, Alice Morley, Helen Flood and Jeannelle Brew. Thank you to Anna at The Woodbine Workshop for the beautiful cover.

Thank you to my parents Yasmin Khan and Riyaz Talkhani. You did not always understand me, but you never let that get in the way of being there for me. This book and this life would not have been possible without your love, support, *duas* and endless sacrifices.

I do not know what I would do without the comforting presence of my siblings Raiyan Talkhani and Rasha Talkhani. You will always be the main characters in my life! It has been a pleasure to share this journey with you and to watch you grow.

To N, my husband, thank you for everything, but mostly, thank you for the joy. *Alhumdulillah*.

Many thanks to everyone at Newgen Publishing UK, I couldn't have written this book without your unconditional support and encouragement from day one. And everyone at ProQuest, especially the CPCM team, who became my home away from home and were there for me when I was at my most vulnerable.

Thank you to my teachers and peers at International Indian School Jeddah, Al Wadi International School Jeddah, Manipal School of Communication, Hochschule Bremen, Anglia Ruskin University and Pembroke's 2013 Creative Writing programme.

Thank you to my friends Tabi Joy, Kris Siosyte, Rija Zia, Shweta V Shetty, Shaheen Kasmani, Hajera Memon, Megan Bull, Areej Peeran, Julia Rodrigues, Ros Attenborough, Fatima Patel, Awijit Paliwal, Chris Boland, Rabiya Momin, Laurida Harrington-Poireau, Alissa El Assaad Dandashi, Shaima Shamsi, Nadine Aisha Jassat, Shagufta K. Iqbal, Vineet Kumar, Tanzeem Naushad, Sabba Khan, Stefan Lakeband and Hiba Shuja.

Thank you to my online family, from blogger and Tumblr to Twitter and Instagram. You are too many to name and that is my good fortune. Thank you for checking up on me, for reading my words, for following my journey and for encouraging me to write this book. Your support keeps me going.

Above all, *Alhumdulillah* for this life, for the lessons, for the opportunities and privileges. *Alhumdulillah* for the good sense to ask *How can I make this better?* instead of giving in to the lament *Why me?*

Join a literary community of
like-minded readers who seek out
the best in contemporary writing.

From the thousands of submissions Sceptre
receives each year, our editors select the books
we consider to be outstanding.

We look for distinctive voices, thought-provoking
themes, original ideas, absorbing narratives and
writing of prize-winning quality.

If you want to be the first to hear about our
new discoveries, and would like the chance to
receive advance reading copies of our books
before they are published, visit

www.sceptrebooks.co.uk

 Follow @sceptrebooks

 'Like' SceptreBooks

Watch SceptreBooks